Beyond
the
Arches

Beyond

the

Arches

UNCOVERING THE POWER
OF **VOCATION** AND **VIRTUE** TO
ACHIEVE EXCELLENCE

John Abbate

BEYOND THE ARCHES

Uncovering the Power of Vocation and Virtue to Achieve Excellence

FIRST EDITION

ISBN 978-1-5445-4599-8 Hardcover
      978-1-5445-4598-1 Paperback
      978-1-5445-4597-4 Ebook
      978-1-5445-4596-7 Audiobook

To my mom:

*For her self-confidence, courage, and love.
As the saying goes, "Behind every good man is a great woman."
That certainly is the case with my mother. Our family journey over
the past fifty-five years would not have been possible without her yes,
her willingness to take a leap of faith from a life of safety and
comfort to my father's vision for our future. When my mother was
sixteen, growing up in the late 1950s, she dreamed of a life as a wife
and mother. She made her dream a wonderful reality for herself,
my father, and our family. She always prided herself on this
beautiful and often overlooked vocation. What a joy and honor
it has been for those of us who have reaped the benefits
of her generosity and talents as a homemaker.*

To my wife:

*In December 2001, my wife, Kaaren, and I attended
a random Christmas party where we ran into a charming older
gentleman my wife knew. He complimented her, saying,
"Young lady, you are as beautiful on the outside as you are on the inside."
It was an innocuous comment, and it made me proud to hear this
about her. I have been subconsciously ruminating on this ever since.
In some small way, his comment was a "mustard seed" that helped
germinate the idea of this book and a tribute to her relentless
desire to project and provide goodness in the world.*

To Luke:

*As fate would have it, at that same Christmas party we
met a young couple named Jen and Steve. They have become
our dearest friends over the past twenty-three years.
A few years after we met them, Jen and Steve had a third child,
Luke, born with Down syndrome. Luke is now nineteen, and
his humor, charm, and kindness continue to demonstrate
the power of authentic beauty, truth, and goodness to transform
the world. I dedicate this book to my godson, Luke, who has
demonstrated these virtues so powerfully for others to witness.
He is also my best McDonald's customer!*

To my brother:

*Last, I dedicate this book to my brother Jim,
who encouraged me to reexamine the idea of inspiration as
a guide in my daily decisions. His wisdom and perspective
on this idea changed the trajectory of my life.
I want to thank him for his love, support, partnership,
and counsel, without which this book
would not have been possible.*

Contents

Introduction

THE YEAR WAS 1969, AND THE UNITED STATES WAS UNDERGOING A significant social and cultural revolution. Events like Woodstock, the Apollo 11 moon landing, the Vietnam War, and the Summer of Love were altering the social fabric of America forever. During this time, my family was to make its own life-altering and radical transformation. My father decided to quit his job as an electrical engineer to become the owner/operator of a fledgling McDonald's franchise in a small farming town in California's Central Valley.

Growing up in a traditional Italian family, my father had never been a fan of fast food and had tasted hamburgers only a few times in his life. He had a good job at General Electric, a wife, and five children under the age of six. We were living close to our extended family and friends. It was the idyllic mid-twentieth century exis-tence in post–World War II suburbia. So when he decided to invest his life savings and future career in an obscure business he knew little about in a dusty rural town away from family and friends, it was a gamble that most people in his life could not comprehend. Even now, some sixty years later, it's hard to fully grasp the audacity that was required to make such a move.

My siblings and I began working at my dad's restaurants as small children and continued throughout high school and college. In 1997, my brother and I chose McDonald's as our life's career path and finalized the process of becoming approved owners. We have been owner/operators of McDonald's restaurants ever since.

As a leader, you know that achieving excellence in business is more challenging today than ever before. Issues like tardiness and frequent absences have become rampant. Employees are often disconnected from their organization's vision, and many are indifferent toward striving for excellence in their personal or professional lives. Some employees have a lackadaisical attitude toward their career aspirations and don't see the value in representing their employer's brand standards. Moreover, depression and mental health problems have seen a staggering increase, leading to issues in the workplace. As McDonald's primarily employs youth and young adults, I have had a forward-looking window into the emerging cultural and social shifts of our society. I have witnessed firsthand the changes in our workforce over the past few generations, and the last four years have been unprecedented; they represent a monumental social alteration that cannot be ignored.

Yet don't despair! I firmly believe that we can overcome these obstacles and get our organizations and people reengaged on the path to excellence. Imagine happier and friendlier employees who enjoy their jobs more, communicate more effectively, and feel more comfortable in a work environment that represents the culture you desire. This can result in low employee turnover, mutual respect, support among coworkers and management, and, ultimately, increased profits or contentment for all stakeholders. This is not an unrealistic dream, but something tangible and aspirational to work toward. This book is full of optimism and encouragement; it is an invitation to approach things differently. By rediscovering and applying the transcendental virtues to your life, organization, and community, you can turn the tide and foster a different culture that can eventually lead to personal and professional excellence.

In this book, you'll learn to listen to the call for a reawakening in your life. You'll gain an understanding of the difference between success and excellence and why you must strive for excellence. You'll get a deeper understanding of our current cultural and social environment and develop tools for operating within it to positively affect your employees, your organization, and the others in your life. You will be encouraged to embrace a different kind of leadership, one led by the transcendental virtues of beauty, truth, and goodness. You will see how to embody these virtues by glimpsing people and organizations that have done so. You will be exposed to a new viewpoint on the power of vocation and how we can strive for excellence even during the most challenging times of life and work.

This book's message is based on my decades of managing dozens of McDonald's restaurants and interacting with thousands of employees who work with me every day. Rarely has a day gone by in the last thirty-two years when I have not been thinking about or discussing the operations and challenges of serving our customers the QSC&V (quality, service, cleanliness, and value) that has been the brand's hallmark for seventy years. The radiance of the golden arches has provided a constant source of motivation, inspiration, and purpose on my journey in search of the ever-elusive "mark of excellence." I've been speaking to folks about many of the topics addressed in this book for years; I wrote this book because I was compelled to share the same wisdom with a broader audience.

"If I had a brick for every time I've repeated
the phrase Quality, Service, Cleanliness and Value,
I think I'd probably be able to bridge the
Atlantic Ocean with them."
—RAY KROC

I also wrote this book to share my story and to encourage you to tell your story as well, because telling our stories is important. The United States is a shining light on a hill and a beacon of hope for the world. It is the freedom, compassion, and collective values that till the soil of prosperity for all of us. Culture and values matter. We must pass on the cultural fabric of our lives. Our lives matter, and our history binds together the very best of our society from generation to generation.

"You begin to liquidate a people by taking away its memory.
You destroy its books, its culture, its history.
And then others write other books for it, give another
culture to it, invent another history for it.
Then the people slowly begin to forget
what it is and what it was."
—MILAN KUNDERA, *The Book of Laughter and Forgetting*

To help you better comprehend the principles I discuss in this book, I use my personal experiences working at McDonald's as a key backdrop. Since most individuals have visited a McDonald's restaurant, watched *The Founder*, starring Michael Keaton, or at least seen McDonald's commercials, I believe it is a perfect reference point to provide clarity and some familiar color.

I use the philosophy of the ancient Greeks, such as Plato and Aristotle, to make the case for a renewed focus on the ageless wisdom in our cultural history as well as the rich biblical narratives that have shaped Western civilization. Regardless of your religious views, you can glean much secular, common-sense wisdom from Scripture that unequivocally applies to modern management theory.

Finally, to inspire you and demonstrate examples of the kind of leadership I am promoting, I've included stories from amazing individuals from diverse backgrounds who are committed to the success of McDonald's and its employees. Their unwavering dedication and enthusiasm are truly inspiring. They view their work as a calling and an opportunity to positively impact the lives of others. Many of them have spent several decades working for McDonald's, driven by a sense of purpose and a strong desire to lead others toward achieving excellence. This "pay it forward" mentality is the essence of authentic leadership. Their stories and perspectives reinforce the power of collective efforts toward achieving personal excellence. At McDonald's, we like to think we are a "team of teams" *arching* for excellence. It is that generous spirit of achievement through community that becomes the long-term cultural success we seek.

> "None of us is as good as all of us."
>
> —RAY KROC

I invite you to challenge your assumptions, opinions, and experiences regarding what constitutes success and use that as a springboard to gain greater insight into your own journey toward seeking personal excellence. Flourishing businesses do not happen by accident; you must choose to implement new ways of thinking and behaving to revitalize your organization. Intrinsic excellence requires you to adapt to change and stay committed to your path. This book proposes that you can achieve your path by harnessing the foundational idea of vocation grounded in the timeless values and wisdom of beauty, truth, and goodness.

CHAPTER 1

A Shout!

"To the hard of hearing you *shout*, and for the almost
blind you draw large and startling figures."
—FLANNERY O'CONNOR

FLANNERY O'CONNOR IS CONSIDERED ONE OF THE MOST INFLU-
ential authors of the twentieth century. Her writing style is characterized by a unique blend of dark humor, vivid imagery, irony,
and obvious religious undertones. She utilized these elements to
expose the shortcomings, hypocrisies, and moral flaws of her char-
acters and society as a whole. When confronted with criticism of
her obtrusive writing style, she famously replied with the above
statement.

I find this famous quip and her work provocative, particularly
when contemplating the COVID-19 pandemic and its aftermath
over the past few years. O'Connor's quote suggests that in a world
that has become excessively distracted by external noise and moral
ambiguity, society requires a proverbial "shout" to awaken our sen-
sibilities and garner our attention. Is it conceivable that God has
utilized this opportunity to make us more mindful of our actions,

beliefs, and priorities? Could this be a personal, professional, and societal wake-up call reminding us of the frailty of life and the importance of relationships, values, and vocation to living a successful and excellent life?[1]

My Personal Reawakening

Looking back at the five years of my life since the release of my previous book, *Invest Yourself*, I can't help but feel a little disenchanted and chagrined about how my professional journey has unfolded. Instead of feeling greater fulfillment and satisfaction, I have faced countless sleepless nights and burdens that were not part of my vision for this career stage. I guess you could say...I thought I had it figured out. This reminds me of the adage "If you want to make God laugh, tell him your plans." The past few years have presented me with numerous challenges that tested my resilience and, in my weaker moments, made me question my commitment to charity and my vocational mission.

A wise mentor once told me to remember that "choices have consequences." Initially, I thought this statement was a simple warning to be cautious about the decisions I make, but as time passed, I began to see its more introspective meaning. It's not the big, life-changing choices we make, like deciding on a career or a financial investment, that determine the course of our lives. Instead, it's the smaller, daily choices we make in response to the unpredictable and uncontrollable events in our lives that truly shape our future.

---

[1] Robert Barron, "Hope during the Coronavirus," March 24, 2020, YouTube video, 31:20, https://youtu.be/L8lVpB6EJJM?si=pnws2o-Kekbx_zUd.

How we choose to handle our mistakes, setbacks, and emotional struggles can have far-reaching consequences that impact not just our lives but those of our loved ones. My mentor's warning is a reminder that every choice we make, no matter how insignificant it may seem, has the power to influence the course of our lives in ways we may not even realize.

Over the past few years, I have made a few investments that proved to be ill-fated and demoralizing, faced frivolous lawsuits that drained our resources, and dealt with massive legislative changes imposed by the state of California that added to my struggles and negativity. However, nothing could have prepared me for the unexpected and unprecedented challenge of the COVID-19 pandemic and its cultural aftermath.

I revisited my journal entries from March 2020 to gain a deeper understanding of my state of mind during those unprecedented times and to paint a vivid picture of the collective consciousness that engulfed the world.

March 8

This coronavirus seems to be taking on a life of its own. It will be very interesting to see what happens over the next month or so. I expect the stock market to get hammered again on Monday. I'm glad I am not overmargined at the moment. It has dropped 3,000 and may go back to 20,000 before things begin to turn again. McDonald's just canceled their Worldwide Convention. It seems like overkill, but I guess you never know.

March 12

Thursday a.m. I was supposed to be in Chicago but canceled due to the coronavirus. The whole world is in turmoil. Markets have crashed, and panic is everywhere. I have never seen anything like it in my lifetime. It's kind of like 9/11 and the market crash of 2008. A shitload of unknowns. So far, our business is okay, but what happens when cases hit the Central Valley? This could get a lot worse. Matthew has a three-week break now. Who knows if not longer? He will drive home now.

I am a bit scared...We are certain of a recession now. It could impact elections as well. Just need to stay calm and keep praying.

March 15

The news continues to be bad...all about the coronavirus. Now ski slopes are closing, and discussions are underway to close bars, restaurants, etc. This could easily happen in the coming week. Spain and France have now done so. The situation is incredibly fluid. Most Catholic churches and other larger gatherings have closed their doors as well. I will have a call tomorrow with the McDonald's system to see what plans they have put into place for the preservation of our restaurants and our financial situation. Sales yesterday were very soft, but not disastrous. Down big on the freeways and Walmart locations again. The news is so bleak...but I know that things will be better at some point. We must continue the faith...and not panic. I'm afraid it will get worse before it gets better. More cases for hysteria to happen. USD [University of San Diego] announced the cancelation of the semester. Sure other schools to follow within the week.

Mass reading today: The gospel from John about Christ and the woman at the well. Living water, the water that will ultimately quench our thirst, is only through HIM and our faith. The older I get…the more that becomes an obvious reality. There really is nothing in this world that can permanently quench our thirst. The first reading is about the Israelites in the desert losing faith in God and Moses. Finally, Moses strikes his staff against a rock to produce water. However, once again the people have lost faith in God and must be shown a sign. In these crazy times…do I have faith in God? We are certainly roaming in the desert at the moment…and must have faith in the ultimate outcome of this craziness.

March 18

What a crazy depressing day. The market dropped drastically again today. I am very worried about liquidity. The restaurants are only open in the DT [drive-thru], basically. Dining rooms closed…

It is one of the scariest periods of my life. The great unknown is terrifying. The news is so depressing. Our locations continue to do okay. Maybe down 15%.

California is now in a "shelter in place" state. Only able to leave your house for essential items, etc. Eventually the whole country as well.

All Masses and services are canceled.

March 21

I can hardly express the fear and anxiety of this moment in time. I could have never imagined this in my lifetime. Truly historic and surreal in scope and depth. Right before dinner last night, I got a text that martial law was to be imposed within 48 to 72 hours. Everything to close but hospitals and absolute essential services. The general of the National Guard refutes, but of course he would. The misinformation is rampant. This is going out of control so fast…God help us all.

Yesterday was a good day at work. Just hunkering down trying to create contingency plans. Trying anything and everything to free up cash to survive this holocaust. Market down again yesterday. Hope we can stay open enough to accumulate a little cash, but not if we have to close our locations. As of today, all WM and mall locations closed. We are in a war…makes no sense to keep them open any longer. Too much risk and hassle for NO money benefit.

March 24

Well…It's been a very tough road. My Sunday was not good. I just immersed in thoughts about the business and COVID-19. Sales were lousy and much unknown. The futures market pointed to a mass sell-off on Monday due to no congressional compromise on a stimulus bill. I was just in a tough frame of mind and too many days working from home and not being very positive…

I have impacted Kaaren and the kids in a very negative way. I have allowed the problems of my business to come out of my mouth and my demeanor. On Monday—Matthew called me out on it. He also called Steve and Doug to vent and to tell them to call me. I have been under a bit of overload trying to prepare for the worst.

March 27

I have been in a bad spot the past couple of weeks with the coronavirus and its impact on our lives. I have had to face continuous anxiety and fear about our health and the health of the economy and our business. It has put me in a state of hyperfocus, isolation, and a very directive mentality. The space for gentleness, kindness, etc., has not really been there while I tried to navigate such unchartered waters. I certainly have not been in a kind or gentle state of mind.

My self-control kicks into overdrive as well. I am trying to remain faithful and trying to do things to allow this to permeate my life.

I feel much calmer now and more in control. I can feel myself becoming more centered but still in a focused and crisis mode. The subjective unknown is certainly hard for me. And the fear of failure...What could or should I have done differently, etc.

As the pandemic swept across the globe in March 2020, it was like a tidal wave crashing down on our business. As part of the McDonald's franchise ownership system, we were immediately hit with a significant and sudden drop in business. Some of our restaurants were forced to shut down completely, and the stress and uncertainty of those early days were overwhelming. I was trying to figure out how to repay the business loans to the banks and pay the fixed rent to McDonald's while calculating the ramifications of COVID-19 on our business and restaurant operations. Although our company was financially strong, cash flow can extend only so far when business drops 40 to 50 percent overnight. If the business were to continue on the same trajectory for the next six months, we would run out of money by the fall.

Furthermore, we were dealing with all the personal protective equipment, health department, and Cal/OSHA mandates in restaurants daily. In times of distress and confusion, my managerial style is directive. This manifested in stern conversations with my staff about what we needed to do and how we needed to perform... *now*. We had Zoom calls every single day, sometimes twice a day, for months to ensure we could get through this challenging time as an organization and make the necessary daily decisions to adapt to an ever-changing business landscape.

As the pandemic accelerated, I struggled to maintain a positive outlook at home. My demeanor was often stern and pessimistic, and I held a hostile attitude and contempt toward governmental policies and politicians. Unfortunately, my wife and children were constantly exposed to this environment of negativity, and it affected them more than I realized. My son, Matthew, who had to return home from college due to the pandemic, was visibly distressed by my behavior and its impact on our family. He was already dealing with his share of pandemic fears and frustrations, and my negativity only added to his burden. One day, without my knowledge, he called one of my closest friends and asked him to talk to me. Matthew thought that my negative outlook was spiraling out of control and that I needed a fresh perspective from someone I trusted to help me see how my disposition was impacting everyone around me.

The call with my friend was a turning point—the "shout" that got my attention. I was sad and a bit ashamed of myself for needing my son to intervene. But it helped me realize how my actions and attitude impacted those around me. I understood how significantly I was affecting the people I loved and the people I counted on at work. My choices had consequences. I had to choose whether to spread optimism or continue to spew pessimism.

From that moment on, I decided to choose positivity and embrace the chaos rather than fear it. I didn't want to weigh down my children and employees with the negativity I was projecting; instead, I needed to inspire them with hope and encouragement. I was not always perfect in the following months, but at least I learned to have enough self-awareness to listen and self-correct. I couldn't control the future, but I could manage my attitude and how I dealt with it, not only with my family but also with my coworkers and staff.

A Professional Reawakening

As I delved deeper into introspection, I began to see the pandemic as a shout that was demanding my attention to the business as a whole. Like all business owners, not only did I personally need to acclimate to a new reality, but I needed to find ways for our organization to change. I gained a better sense of the need for innovative thinking to find more effective ways to lead and inspire individuals in the rapidly changing world.

Managing a business like McDonald's can be highly complex. Each establishment has anywhere from fifty to a hundred employees, all with unique personalities, motivations, mental health issues, work ethics, experiences, and cognitive abilities. Since the COVID-19 pandemic, managing the human aspect of the business has become even more challenging. Most of the operational issues we face are due to complex "human capital" problems rather than our complicated systems of production or service. McDonald's is a labor-intensive business that requires a high degree of synergy and cooperation, so if even one or two people are missing from a shift, delivering on our QSC&V philosophy becomes almost impossible. Unfortunately, most McDonald's locations nationwide are now missing several people per day who simply choose not to show up to work, leading to significant challenges in maintaining the quality and consistency of our products. Automation is not the solution. Like many other businesses, at McDonald's, human interaction and employee cooperation tend to be the "secret ingredient" for success.

What worked for or inspired our employees ten, five, or even three years ago is no longer as effective today. This may be due to temporal factors, such as too much government stimulus, or longer-term trends, such as changes in mental health and cultural values regarding work and sacrifice. Either way, status quo management will not fix the issue. Our workforce has undergone a remarkable transformation in recent years, with a shift in priorities, self-perception, work ethic, and outlook toward the future. As leaders, we must be willing to acknowledge this reality and seek solutions.

A Cultural Reawakening

After spending considerable time pondering COVID-19's chain of events and its legacy from several angles, I've come to believe that the pandemic and its aftermath are also shouting at us as a culture.

> "All gave some and some gave all."
>
> —BILLY RAY CYRUS

The song "Some Gave All" by Billy Ray Cyrus is about the Vietnam War. For me, the lyrics carry a powerful message and make a thought-provoking connection between the social and political unrest of the Vietnam War era and the challenges faced during and in the aftermath of the pandemic. Many of us have lost loved ones, and all of us have experienced some degree of loss through restrictions on our liberties, our social interactions, and our sense of safety and security.

> "Ignorance leads to fear, fear leads to hatred,
> and hatred leads to violence."
> —IBN RUSHD

The past four years have been marked by a series of tumultuous events that have showcased both the best and the worst of humanity. We have witnessed everything from the panic buying of essential supplies like toilet paper to widespread protests and demonstrations calling for the defunding of police, justifying looting, and highlighting the deep-seated class divide in our society. Our legislative environment has become more toxic and subversive. Lack of governmental transparency, spread of misinformation, and constant fearmongering have fueled hatred and violence, leading to a breakdown in relationships at both the personal and societal levels. Having a civil conversation with friends and family who hold opposing views on these topics has become increasingly challenging, making it clear we are living in truly unprecedented times.

> "Thinking is difficult. Therefore, let the
> herd pronounce judgment!"
> —CARL JUNG

Furthermore, in our isolation during the lockdown, we became increasingly reliant on social media, and with the release of ChatGPT in 2022, artificial intelligence (AI) began to catch on with the general public and has been snowballing ever since. The impact of social media and AI on our lives, especially those of the younger generation, is a matter of great concern. These technologies' ability to be exploited to attract and influence people to mass conformity is terrifying. Sociologists have done well-documented research highlighting the negative consequences of excessive social media usage on our children. There is no simple vaccine to immunize ourselves against this issue; we must consider ways to find a solution.

What Now?

We've been woken up by the shout of the pandemic and its aftermath. What can we do about it? The path to joy and contentment in our postmodern, social-media-focused, and AI-dominated world is challenging but worth pursuing. We must rediscover a vision for life that is not skewed or manipulated by the filters of social media or the distortion of our cultural dysfunction.

Now is the time to ask ourselves: Prior to "social distancing," was I pursuing excellence in my personal life and organization? Was I exercising the opportunity to be in meaningful communion with friends, family, and coworkers? How was I prioritizing my time? Most importantly, how can I change gears and begin to achieve success by striving for intrinsic excellence?

"Courage is the management of and the triumph over fear.
It's the decision—in a moment of peril, or day in and
day out—to take ownership, to assert agency,
over a situation, over yourself, over the fate that
everyone else has resigned themselves to.
We can curse the darkness, or we can light a candle."
—WALT WHITMAN

By embracing the ancient wisdom of our past, we can move beyond the fear and physical superficiality that have become so prevalent in our age. This takes courage, introspection, and a leap of faith.

CHAPTER 2

Success versus Excellence

"Pursue excellence and success will follow."

—AUSTIN GEORGE

THIS BOOK IS ABOUT ACHIEVING EXCELLENCE, YET I HAVE USED THE word *success* a few times over the course of these first pages. Before delving further, I want to make sure I define this word as it relates back to a view of ourselves. *Success* and *excellence* are often used interchangeably, but they are quite distinct from one another. Success is generally based on how you compare to others and indicates an assessment at the conclusion of a journey. It is usually used to define the pursuit of external status, power, prestige, wealth, and privilege. On the other hand, excellence is based on your own intrinsic potential and is measured against your own standards. It is the pursuit of quality in one's work and effort, whether the culture recognizes it or not. It is not a report card at the end of your journey.[2]

---

[2] "Pursue Excellence and Success Will Follow," Success Minded, December 6, 2022, https://successminded.co/pursue-excellence-and-success-will-follow/.

Living a life of intrinsic excellence is about constantly striving to improve oneself. It involves pursuing positive thoughts and actions that lead to gradual improvement. It requires asking oneself questions such as *Will I be better tomorrow than I am today?* and *Will I be more thoughtful, intentional, and purposeful in the future than I am right now?* By focusing on excellence rather than success, you can achieve true fulfillment and happiness in life.

We have a common tendency to fall into the trap of comparing ourselves to others. We often find ourselves thinking about what others have accomplished or the things they own, and we can't help feeling envious or jealous. This mindset is particularly pervasive among some owner/operators in the McDonald's world who are constantly comparing themselves to one another and competing to own the most restaurants to achieve the elusive idea of success. However, based on my experience...most never find it.

Unfortunately, the comparison mindset can hold us back from realizing our true potential. We become so focused on what others are doing that we lose sight of our own path to excellence. However, there is a way to break free from these shackles and reach our full potential. By embracing beauty, truth, and goodness, we can shift our focus to our own path to excellence and become the best version of ourselves.

Of course, this doesn't mean that life will always be easy. We'll encounter challenges and sorrows along the way, and sometimes we have to accept them and carry on. But by staying true to our own path, we can find a sense of purpose and fulfillment that goes beyond the shallow comparison game.

Two people come to mind when I consider the success versus excellence paradigm.

Elon Musk

In late 2023, Walter Isaacson's latest book on tech guru and prolific businessman Elon Musk left a deep impression on me. Having read countless biographies and autobiographies, I found Musk's character different from that of anyone I had ever encountered. His persona is intriguing and fascinating, yet disturbing. Despite his massive achievements and success, he seems deeply unhappy, and his life has been a constant battle. He may well be the most restless and tragic figure of our time, driven by a relentless pursuit to fill the emptiness in his heart and soul with temporal tapestries of this world while masquerading as the world's savior. He wages a war within himself and the secular world, and his intentions and the outcome remain perpetually unclear. He believes his intelligence can find the answers, but he continues to ask himself the wrong questions or seek the wrong outcomes. Musk is a caricature of the modern man, and his life is a parody worthy of a *Saturday Night Live* sketch. He chases a ghost, maybe his own ghost. As St. Thomas More says in the play *A Man for All Seasons*, "it profit a man nothing to give his soul for the whole world... but for Wales?" The sentiment still holds true today. In Musk's case, he seems to be doing just that, all in the pursuit of... Mars!

We cannot compare ourselves to the likes of Elon Musk in terms of success. But if we abandon the notion of success as the measure of our worth, we can all strive for excellence in our vocational journey. Even though Musk may be considered the greatest *success* story of our generation, his *excellence* is still up for debate. I work in the fast-food industry, and I know I won't be the one to solve the world's problems or lead us to Mars. However, I can make a difference in my chosen profession, and that impact is what makes all the difference to me. Will I eventually obtain "success"? Well, that depends on whom you compare me to and how you define success. However, nobody but me can hold me back from pursuing excellence.

> "If you want to change the world, start with yourself."
> —MOHANDAS GANDHI

A Fortunate Pilgrim

My grandfather is a direct contrast to the Elon Musks of the world. Born on the beautiful but very deprived island of Sicily in 1903, he left his homeland, like many of his generation, to begin a new life in America. He left behind his mother and father, would not be able to return to his homeland for forty years, and would never see his father again. My grandfather arrived in America on February 28, 1921, through the Port of Boston, and then took a train to Pueblo, Colorado, to get a job working in a steel mill. Over the course of time, he would eventually end up in Ohio, working for Firestone Tire and Rubber Company. He spent most of his working years as a simple laborer, managing to eke out a living for himself, his wife, and their seven children. They lived on a small farm just outside of town in a two-bedroom farmhouse with no indoor plumbing. To supplement his income, my grandfather raised chickens and pigs and took up gardening. He became skilled at growing a variety of fruits and vegetables, and his children sold his produce around the neighborhood. This helped him make ends meet and provided the family with a sense of pride and accomplishment on their little farm in the midst of the Depression and the mandated rationing during World War II.

Despite his own limited opportunities, my grandfather dreamed of a better life for his children. He believed that education was the key to a brighter future, and he encouraged his children to pursue their studies and acquire the skills needed to succeed in life. He was convinced the trades were the key to a successful career. He sent his boys to a vocational high school to make sure they entered the workplace with a marketable skill. My two uncles became amazing machinists, mastering a skillset that provided solid career opportunities over their lifetimes. My own father went to college; he was one of the very few from his vocational high school who did so.

Was my grandfather successful? Well, he certainly was never financially successful, nor did he ever obtain worldly power, prestige, or honor. Yet he was one of the most extraordinary figures in my life and in the lives of many others. His life was one of consistent beauty, truth, and goodness. He saw beauty in nature; his garden; the Italian food he loved; his wife, Angela; his Catholic faith; and his children and grandchildren. He stood for truth in his unwavering commitment to the American idea, the truth and teachings of his Catholic faith, and the truth of what it means to be a moral and righteous husband and father. His beauty and truth became an incredible goodness as the foundation for the success of his children, grandchildren, and great-grandchildren. You could say his values were the inheritance that he left his children, and they were passed on from generation to generation.

So, while my grandfather may not have been "successful" per society's definition, he led an exemplary life of personal excellence, and his legacy has few boundaries.

CHAPTER 3

The Shadows We Cast

"Knowing your shadow self is vital if you wish
to bring harmony into your life."
—CARL JUNG

To fully comprehend this book's central message—that we discover our excellence by practicing the ancient transcendental virtues—we must first delve more deeply into the importance of our existence in relation to society. Rarely do our actions reside in isolation; instead, they tend to reverberate across time and space. How we relate to others and how they perceive us greatly affects the degree to which we can achieve excellence.

"The shadow you cast" is a psychological concept originating from the Swiss psychiatrist and psychoanalyst Carl Jung. According to Jung, the shadow operates in the realm of the subconscious, influencing our thoughts, behaviors, and emotions. It determines the persona we present to others, and when we suppress the undesirable aspects of ourselves, we tend to cast those negative self-perceptions onto others. In the physical world, for a shadow to be cast, an object must obstruct a path of light. In Jung's analogy, it is the light of our lives that exposes our shadows to the world. Jung's concept has been adapted and expressed in various ways. Today, the shadow is used as a metaphor to describe the power of our influence upon others. The depth of our awareness of our shadow self determines whether we cast a positive or negative shadow.

Daniel, director of strategy and integration for a McDonald's owner/operator, explains why this concept is important to leaders in particular:

We as leaders cast a shadow. Your shadow touches somebody's life. What kind of shadow are you casting? You've got to be that representative. You've got to be that person that's going to positively influence other people's lives to make them better. If you're doing anything else, you're doing the wrong thing. That's not what I want you to do. Whether you realize it or not, you're influencing your people and customers. They're a victim of their environments. So give them a good memory of McDonald's. I don't want them walking away with a bad memory. I don't care if they quit, saying, "It's not for me," but I want them to end that sentence with, "thank you." And I want you to reply, "Hey, okay, but I hope to see you in the drive-thru. You came in here as a customer. You're going out as a customer. You better say hi when you come back in." Let them leave on good terms.

The shadows of our interior beings cannot be concealed. We reveal them to the world, unknowingly. We all cast shadows all the time. The question is not whether you cast a shadow, but rather how positive or negative it is. Every day, I look in the mirror and remind myself of this reality. It is that important.

Before we can find our excellence, we must face the dilemma of the shadow—by first acknowledging its existence and then understanding it in the context of projection, attraction, culture, conformity, and fragility.

Projection

Many metaphors can be used to describe our internal lives, but I believe the most fitting is the image of battle. In this interior battle, our own self can either be our greatest ally or our sternest opponent. There is a dynamic tension between the elements of our personality that drive us toward personal growth and those that hold us back. Each one of us must deal with the potential for both good and evil that resides within us. Whether our strengths and capacity for good prevail or our weaknesses and capacity for evil gain the upper hand depends on the outcome of the battle that rages within us. St. Paul spoke of exactly this struggle more than two thousand years ago.

"I do not understand the things I do.
I do not do what I want to do, and I do the things I hate.
And if I do not want to do the hated things I do, that means
I agree that the law is good. But I am not really the one who
is doing these hated things; it is sin living in me that does
them. Yes, I know that nothing good lives in me—
I mean nothing good lives in the part of me that is earthly
and sinful. I want to do the things that are good, but I do
not do them. I do not do the good things I want to do,
but I do the bad things I do not want to do. So if I do things
I do not want to do, then I am not the one doing them.
It is sin living in me that does those things."
—ST. PAUL'S Letter to the Romans 7:15–20 (New Century Version)

Unfortunately, many of us refuse to acknowledge the negative aspects of our personalities and use psychological defense mechanisms to remain ignorant of our faults and weaknesses. This, as we learned from Jung, results in negative shadows. Our subconscious self-criticism causes us to treat others poorly or engage in self-destructive behavior. Instead of taking responsibility for our actions, we project onto the innocent to avoid confronting our shadows.

> "Projection is one of the commonest psychic phenomena . . .
> Everything that is unconscious
> in ourselves we discover in our neighbor,
> and we treat him accordingly."
>
> —CARL JUNG, "Archaic Man," *Modern Man in Search of a Soul*

At times we encounter people who project intensely negative energy upon us instead of owning their own failings. Often we catch ourselves doing the same. Chances are it is the internal shadow of our being that is driving the negativity rather than some external dynamic. The ugliness and fear within us are projected onto others as a means to avoid facing our own demons.

If we don't confront or acknowledge our innate malevolence—such as internal strife, greed, and envy—these qualities, desires, emotions, and behaviors can have a significant impact on our lives and the lives of others. Good leadership includes being aware of these inner feelings and how they cause us to interact with others.

The Law of Attraction

> "We don't need magic to transform our world.
> We carry all of the power we need inside ourselves already."
>
> —J. K. ROWLING

Understanding and working with the law of attraction helps us shape the shadows we cast. This concept suggests that our focus, thoughts, consumption of material, and conversations influence what we attract to ourselves and project onto others. Electromagnetic charges initiated by our thoughts permeate our bodies and dictate our attractions. In simple terms, the things we give our attention to are the things we'll see more of in our lives. The more we immerse ourselves in particular ideas, media platforms, and thought patterns, the more we become attracted and attached to them and eventually project them onto others.

This law is a powerful force that shapes our lives in numerous ways. Its impact can be observed in our daily routines, our relationships with others, and the overall direction of our lives. For example, as my son brought to my attention during the pandemic, I was consumed by fear and negativity, which I then projected onto others, and this led to increased pessimism around me—thus impacting my community.

According to recent estimates, 6,200 thoughts run through the average person's mind per day. Shockingly, most of these thoughts —around 80 percent—are negative, and a whopping 95 percent are repetitive. It's crucial to consider the impact of this constant mental chatter on our daily lives and how it intersects with the law of attraction.[3]

Many times, I have found myself drawn toward the negatives associated with my business instead of focusing on its positive elements. In the early stages of my career, I would feel frustrated

---

[3] NeuroGym Team, "New Study: You Have 6,200 Thoughts a Day... Don't Make Yours Negative," accessed June 2, 2024, https://blog.myneurogym.com/new-study-you-have -6900-thoughts-a-day-dont-make-yours-negative/.

and pessimistic when I arrived at a restaurant location with a slow-moving drive-thru line. My negative energy would permeate the restaurant, making the situation even worse. If I had only looked at the situation differently, assuming positivity and innocence rather than negativity, I could have taken the opportunity to improve the service and show gratitude for the business. This shift in perspective would have created a more helpful outcome. But making that shift requires shadow awareness and an understanding of the concept and implication of the law of attraction on others.

A few years back, my wife and I attended a marriage workshop led by Dr. Allen Hunt, the author of *The 21 Undeniable Secrets of Marriage*. Dr. Hunt introduced us to the work of Dr. John Gottman, a renowned psychologist and researcher on relationships and marriage. Gottman is known for his work using a five-to-one ratio to predict marital and relationship stability. This ratio pertains to the balance of positive and negative interactions within a relationship. Gottman's research suggests that for a relationship to thrive and remain stable, the parties involved must have at least five positive interactions for every one negative interaction. He emphasizes that a healthy relationship is not devoid of conflict but is instead characterized by the ability to navigate conflicts constructively while prioritizing positive interactions and sustaining emotional connections. His work highlights the importance of maintaining a significantly higher number of positive experiences, gestures, communications, and interactions than negative ones. Positive interactions can include acts of kindness, support, affection, humor, empathy, understanding, and appreciation. Negative interactions might involve criticism, sarcasm, defensiveness, contempt, stonewalling, or outright hostility.

Gottman's research goes hand in hand with the law of attraction. Positivity attracts the positive, and negativity attracts an even greater negative. I believe the five-to-one ratio concept applies to all relationships, not just marriage. I began applying it to my relationships with my peers and subordinates at work and have seen great improvement.

By actively seeking the positive, we begin to be more positive, and thus we project more positive shadows on others.

The Law of Conformity

As social beings, humans tend to conform to the attitudes, beliefs, and behaviors of those around them, a phenomenon known as conformity. In other words, environment often trumps will. Conformity can manifest in various ways, ranging from explicit social pressure to more subtle subconscious influence. Regardless of its form, conformity wields considerable power. It can alter the behavior of entire groups and impact numerous other aspects of social life.

> "If you sleep with dogs, you will get fleas."
> —MY NANA

The law of conformity acknowledges the powerful force of conformity and suggests we can use it to our advantage, allowing us to wield social power and influence. We can do so more quickly by leveraging the law of attraction with the law of conformity. By consistently demonstrating positive leadership qualities and emitting positive energy, we can shape our cultural environment in a way that promotes conformity to positive values. Conversely, negative leadership and energy can also have a strong impact, leading to conformity to negative behaviors and beliefs.

There seems to be no greater evidence of this phenomenon than the events that spiraled out of control in Washington, DC, on January 6, 2021. Everyone, regardless of political ideology, can recognize that the attack on the Capitol that day is a classic example of the power of influence and attraction to create rapid and dangerous social conformity. The insurrection was irrational, with no real end game. It was the by-product of manipulated emotion and frustration, leading to an unfortunate conclusion for far too many people.

Another example of the law of conformity is found in "prime time." As I write this book, Deion Sanders has taken the sports world by storm as he seeks to transform the University of Colorado football team into a winning program. With his natural charisma, charm, and notoriety, Sanders has captivated the state and much of the country, creating mass conformity to his mission. Since his arrival, the school's lowly football program has become popular and lucrative. He has leveraged the laws of attraction and conformity to maximize his wealth and the fan base for the University of Colorado. Ultimately, for Sanders to be successful over the long term, he must transform raw conformity and attraction into a winning culture.

I recently revisited the miniseries *Band of Brothers*, which centers on E Company, a paratrooper unit in the 101st Airborne Division during World War II. This series offers a compelling illustration of the dynamics related to the laws of attraction and conformity. One notable example of attraction lies in Major Winters, a remarkable leader who had the ability to inspire others to emulate his selfless courage. His leadership showcases the influence of attraction: his character and actions draw others to strive for the same level of bravery. Conformity is seen in the devolvement of morals the E Company soldiers eventually experience. They find themselves immersed in an environment filled with brutality, death, and hatred. Over time, this pervasive environment leads to a gradual transformation in their behavior and attitudes, culminating in their own acts of brutality and even murder.

The series serves as a thought-provoking case study, highlighting how both the attraction of exemplary leadership and the conforming influence of a challenging environment can profoundly shape human behavior and interactions.

The law of conformity combines with the law of attraction to influence the shadows we cast. As we intentionally project positive attitudes, beliefs, and behaviors in our environments, we cast more positive shadows, and the people around us begin to conform. As they adopt the same attitudes, beliefs, and behaviors, we experience even more positivity in our day-to-day lives and thus project even more positive shadows.

Culture

To best leverage the laws of attraction and conformity in your organization, you must consider culture. As humans, we are constantly attracted to things and people while we simultaneously try to avoid or escape certain situations. This natural human tendency creates an opening for leadership, in both a positive and a negative sense, and is responsible for shaping culture. Culture is a crucial driving force for society and organizations. Successful organizations have strong cultures, which great leaders shape. Conversely, we often find that unsuccessful organizations lack strong cultures.

> "Culture eats strategy for breakfast."
> —PETER DRUCKER

Culture is an intricate, diverse, and influential construct that holds immense power. It is a fundamental aspect of what leaders aim to achieve for long-term results, and it all comes back to the essence of this ancient word. To comprehend its complexity and value, we must delve into its etymology and explore its roots. The term *culture* originated from the Latin word *colunt*, which connoted the concepts of worship, cherish, till, or cultivate. At its core, culture was about man's connection with existence. In an agrarian and polytheistic religious framework, *colunt* encapsulated the essence of what it meant to live in harmony with nature.

According to ancient Greek beliefs, Demeter, the goddess of harvest and fertility of the Earth, taught humanity the art of growing and harvesting, which led to the development of farming. This belief formed the foundation of a cultural relationship between society and Demeter. People worshipped, cherished, and made sacrifices for Demeter, and in return, she facilitated a harmonious relationship between man and nature.

As society transitioned from an agrarian economy and a polytheistic world, the meaning of *colunt* underwent a transformation. It evolved from referring to the cultivation of relationships with Demeter and the land to referring to the cultivation of relationships with one another. Culture became a collaborative social construct that emphasizes the cultivation of human interactions and emotions.

Today, culture is a diverse tapestry of beliefs, values, customs, and traditions passed down from generation to generation. It is a reflection of our collective identity, and it influences the way we think, feel, and behave. Understanding culture is of utmost importance in building bridges between different groups of people and fostering greater comprehension, empathy, and respect in our society. One of the great Christian authors of the twentieth century sums up the power and fragility of culture in a profound way:

"Culture, as its name denotes, is an artificial product.
It is like a city that has been built up laboriously
by the work of successive generations, not a jungle which
has grown up spontaneously by the blind pressure
of natural forces. It is the essence of culture that it is
communicated and acquired, and although it is
inherited by one generation from another, it is a social
not a biological inheritance, a tradition of learning,
an accumulated capital of knowledge and a
community of 'folkways' into which the
individual has to be initiated."
—CHRISTOPHER DAWSON

Dawson's point is that culture is a laborious endeavor and a by-product of men's and women's initiative, commitment, and leadership. Yet it is a temporal and fragile organism, one that can be transformed through the laws of attraction and conformity. In today's instantaneous digital world, culture is as delicate and manipulative as it ever has been in our history. The right influencer can shift the thoughts and behaviors of our youth within hours.

The top social media influencers in the world have around 500 million followers! Taylor Swift can move our culture in an instant with her fan base and loyal admirers. She casts a massive shadow across culture, which has both positive and negative potential.

In today's business and marketing landscape, the law of conformity and the impact of social media influence cannot be ignored. As someone who operates within this environment, I have witnessed firsthand the immense effect it can have. In recent years, McDonald's capitalized on conformity and culture in its promotion of the Cactus Jack meal, which was heavily endorsed by the famous rapper and influencer Travis Scott. The strategy proved to be a game changer for the company, resulting in one of its most successful marketing campaigns of all time.

> "Brand is just a perception, and perception
> will match reality over time. Sometimes it will be ahead,
> other times it will be behind. But brand is simply a
> collective impression some have about a product."
> —ELON MUSK, CEO of Tesla Motors

The media strategy of today's McDonald's is quite different than it was just a decade ago. Previously, the advertising budget focused mainly on general market television, radio, and outdoor billboard ads. Today, 85 percent of the marketing budget is directed toward digital media and the use of influencers to create the necessary reach and frequency to drive business growth. Thanks to the power of influencers and social media, the McDonald's brand has been revitalized over the last few years. A brand's image is about collective perception. Aligning with influencers like Travis Scott is making the McDonald's brand more relevant for a new generation of consumers.

Using cultural influencers for marketing simply leverages the principles of conformity and attraction. This approach is highly effective in making messages more memorable and impactful to consumers, ultimately leading to a higher inclination for consumer adoption.

CHAPTER 4

The Fragility of
Our Times

"Difficulty is what wakes up the genius."

—NASSIM NICHOLAS TALEB, *Antifragile*

UNDERSTANDING AND WORKING WITH THE SHADOWS WE CAST IS critical for achieving excellence, and part of doing so is confronting the modern reality of our human fragility. We heard Daniel's take on casting shadows in the previous chapter. In his interview, he also addressed human fragility:

> I've fired people for poor performance or stealing. They know you got them with the goods and you're not going to press charges. You're not going to throw them in jail; you're going to terminate their employment. What they did was wrong and, depending on how old they are and their life experience, you may leave them with a little coaching. "Listen," you might say, "you're gonna get another job after this. You made a mistake here. It's not gonna show up on any criminal record. Don't make that mistake again because you have potential. We saw

greatness in you." (Usually those that steal are the best performers. Because they are good, they think they can get away with it, that they are somehow a step above everybody else.) You might say, "We saw you heading to even higher heights, and we were very pleased with your performance. But because of what you did, we can't keep you on board. I'm sorry, you're being fired. But, listen, I know you're still going to stop and say hi. I don't hold grudges. Life's life. You learn from me, you move on. I hope that's what you do."

I'm not the guy that's going to say "You're fired so get out of here right now!" That just doesn't happen. It is what it is. You don't be an ass about it, and you do want their money as a customer to come back. I don't want them eating somewhere miles away from here. I still want to see them in my drive-thru as a customer. They're going to go to McDonald's anyway, so leave on good terms so they'll go to mine.

Recently a girl we see as a future leader got into a physical fight. The guy that she reports to asked me, "Daniel, how should I handle this?"

"Listen," I said, "there were no charges pressed against anybody. Unfortunately, that's what it is. The only thing I want you to do is coach and mentor her because she's a young person, and fighting was just a reaction. It shouldn't have happened. How can we help her learn from this? We don't tolerate it at all. But what can you do to help change her life to make her better so it doesn't happen again? If you want me to get involved, I'll get involved." I gave him the guidance, now I'll let him do what he does and then I'll certainly follow up with it.

Sometimes you have to be a mentor and you have to help others understand the bigger picture. Again, we don't know what her life experiences were up to this point. Maybe that's how her parents treated her every time there was a confrontation. I don't know. So you have to gather the information. You have to seek first to understand, then to be understood.

Good or bad, the shadow you cast will stick with them one way or another. They're going to talk positively or negatively about their experience. There's no in-between. I want them to say, "I loved working at McDonald's. Our bosses were so good. We were stepping it up; they were disciplined and kicked our butts." That's why I'm like that today as a coach and as a teacher.

Daniel acknowledges the fragility of all humans and suggests we should, therefore, give each other grace in our interactions. He also points out that doing so is good for business.

Antifragility

"A Stoic is someone who transforms fear into prudence,
pain into transformation, mistakes into initiation,
and desire into undertaking."
—NASSIM NICHOLAS TALEB

Conversely, while we acknowledge human fragility, we can also strive to build antifragility. Nassim Nicholas Taleb coined the term *antifragility* in his book *Antifragile*, published in 2012. He uses the term to describe systems or entities that not only withstand shocks, randomness, and disorder but benefit and improve from them. Taleb argued that many natural and human-made systems, including biological organisms, economies, and ideas, exhibit varying degrees of antifragility. He asserts that individuals and societies can benefit from exposure to various viewpoints and experiences, enabling them to adapt and learn from different perspectives. His hypothesis reminds me of my ninety-five-year-old uncle, who often says, "What our country needs is a good depression to toughen us back up."

In order to conquer the obstacles that life throws at us, we must cultivate a combination of mental and physical toughness. Angela Duckworth's book *Grit* makes a case for the importance of qualities like bravery, persistence, and adaptability. By cultivating these types of traits, we can weather the storm and emerge stronger on the other side.

Decreasing Resilience

I used to be convinced that humans are resilient and can withstand far more hardship than they might think. Yet has social media, the pandemic, and instant news changed us? There are growing concerns about our resilience as a community. The constant flow of negative information may have overwhelmed our cognitive capacity, making us more vulnerable to mental fragility. Experts argue that continuous access to information has created an entire generation of emotionally fragile individuals. San Diego State University psychology professor Jean Twenge has conducted extensive research on social media's impact on the well-being of young adults and teenagers who have never known a world without smartphones. Her findings indicate that social media and smartphones have caused significant psychological harm to an entire generation. In her book *iGen*, she explores the effects of modern technology on today's super-connected kids, revealing that they are growing up less happy than previous generations and utterly unprepared for adulthood.

I read an article in the *New York Times* titled "People in Their 20s Aren't Supposed to Be This Unhappy," which discussed the findings of David Blanchflower from the Centers for Disease Control and Prevention.[4] The article revealed that depression has been increasing since 2011, particularly among young women. Over the past decade, these women have experienced 140 percent more depressive episodes, and since 2019, their mental health has worsened by 120 percent.

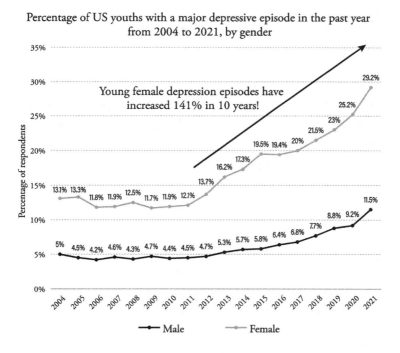

Percentage of US youths with a major depressive episode in the past year from 2004 to 2021, by gender

[4] Peter Coy, "People in Their 20s Aren't Supposed to Be This Unhappy," *New York Times*, September 27, 2023. https://www.nytimes.com/2023/09/27/opinion/mental-health-20s-wellness.html.

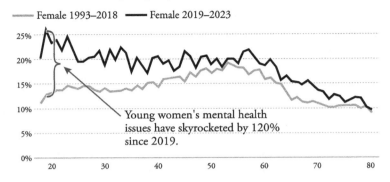

Young Women's Mental Health Has Worsened the Most
Share reporting no good days in past 30 days, by age

Female 1993–2018 ——— Female 2019–2023

Young women's mental health issues have skyrocketed by 120% since 2019.

It's noteworthy that the rise of social media coincided with these trends. Around 2010–2011, social media gained significant popularity and became an essential part of our culture, especially for young people and women. These findings emphasize the clear correlation between the surge in social media usage and its impact on relationships and mental health.

> "The logic of worldly success rests on a fallacy:
> the strange error that our perfection depends on the
> thoughts and opinions and applause of other men!
> A weird life it is, indeed, to be living always in somebody
> else's imagination, as if that were the only place
> in which one could at last become real!"
>
> —THOMAS MERTON

Comparison culture has become a pervasive issue in our society, fueled by the prevalence of social media. The digital age has brought a constant barrage of images and messages that encourage us to compare ourselves to others, even though what we see on social media is often a curated and unrealistic reality. As a result, many individuals find themselves struggling with a range of negative thoughts and emotions, including feelings of inadequacy, poor body image, low self-esteem, and a sense of hopelessness or despair.

These negative thoughts can take many forms, from the belief that "I'm not good enough" to the conviction that "other people have it so much better than me." Negativity due to comparison might manifest as feelings of being overweight, unattractive, or unintelligent or as a pervasive sense of helplessness or the belief that one has bad luck. For some, these thoughts may be so overwhelming that they feel incapable of making any positive changes in their lives, leading to a sense of resignation or despair.

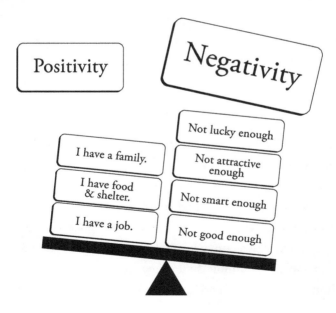

Despite the fact that we have greater access to fundamental necessities such as food, shelter, employment, and material goods than at any other point in history, our society is fraught with discontent. The wealth of a nation like the United States does not insulate us from the damaging effects of comparing ourselves to others and the pressure to meet unattainable expectations. Moreover, we are now instantly aware of any tragedy occurring anywhere in the world. We are constantly exposed to the chaos, sorrow, and cruelty that humanity is capable of, regardless of whether it directly affects us or not. We are bombarded with news about natural disasters and information (and misinformation!) surrounding critical topics such as climate change, pandemics, and the rise of AI.

The overwhelming amount of information we are exposed to on a constant basis is challenging for our minds and emotions to process effectively. Our biological makeup isn't equipped to handle the sheer scope and complexity of the messages we are bombarded with, causing our brains difficulties in finding constructive and positive ways to interpret and respond to them.

Body Chemistry

To better understand why we are more fragile today than ever, we must understand the way the brain works in the face of negativity. Our thoughts have a profound impact on our brain chemistry and basic physiology. Our bodies are programmed to respond in certain ways to different situations, as determined by the limbic system: a set of structures in the brain that deal with emotions and memory. The limbic system regulates function in response to emotional thoughts and is involved in reinforcing behavior. In other words, based on your appraisal of or thoughts about a given situation, your brain has a specific chemical reaction that tells your body how to respond.

The Limbic System

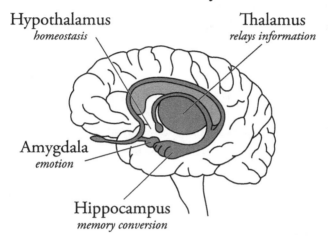

Hypothalamus
homeostasis

Thalamus
relays information

Amygdala
emotion

Hippocampus
memory conversion

The amygdala is an almond-shaped structure in the temporal lobe of the brain that governs the emotional state. This tiny brain structure is responsible for processing both positive emotions, like happiness, and negative ones, like fear and anxiety.

When you have emotionally charged thoughts, your brain releases chemicals, electrical transmissions pass through the brain, and your limbic system takes over. This diverts energy away from your prefrontal cortex, the part of the brain used for cognitive functioning and organization, so you cannot think as clearly. When your thoughts are negative, the chemicals your brain releases are negative and negatively impact you, physically and mentally. This chain reaction happens instantly.[5]

Human brains developed with this biological survival mechanism to protect people from periodic danger. However, the brain does not differentiate between immediate, life-threatening dangers, like being physically attacked, and more innocuous "dangers," like being criticized or hearing about others' misfortunes. Our limbic reality was not developed for social media and massive consumption of negative news.

Antifragility Strategies

"Emotions are data, they are not directives."

—SUSAN DAVID, Emotional Agility

To become less fragile, we must slay the dragon of negativity and its impact on mental health. We must regulate negativity from outside sources as much as possible. This means "fasting" from the people, media platforms, and habits that do not bring us joy and contentment and instead surrounding ourselves with those that do. Ask yourself, "Am I consuming social media, or is it consuming me?"

Learning how to manage our emotions and negative self-talk is crucial. It's important to distinguish between fleeting thoughts and those that can withstand scrutiny. Our brains can create misleading stories based on our personal history or consumed information. For example, seeing only "happy and successful" people on social

---

[5] Daniel G. Amen, *Change Your Brain, Change Your Life: The Breakthrough Program for Conquering Anxiety, Depression, Obsessiveness, Anger, and Impulsiveness* (New York: Harmony, 2015), 91, 110, 111.

media enjoying lives full of fun and vacations can make us believe that this is the reality for everyone...except us.

Susan David's book *Emotional Agility* provides helpful insights on how we can manage our emotions effectively and overcome our fragility and emotional impulses. She emphasizes the importance of being adaptable to our thoughts and feelings, allowing us to respond constructively to any obstacles that come our way. Instead of avoiding challenging emotions or becoming stuck in them, she suggests that we approach them with curiosity and compassion and learn to accept the discomfort that they bring.

> "Choose courage over comfort...Recognize that life's *beauty* is inseparable from its fragility."
> —SUSAN DAVID, *Emotional Agility*

David emphasizes the benefit of perceiving emotions neutrally instead of labeling them as positive or negative. This helps us analyze our thoughts objectively, leading to a better understanding of their validity. Emotionally charged thoughts may not always be based on reality. By examining them logically over time, we can ensure a more accurate evaluation and make better decisions that align with our values. David's book reminds us that our lives are filled with a never-ending cycle of External stimulus → Internal *choice* → Internal/External response. We cannot always control or avoid the stimulus, but ultimately, we can make a choice that manages our response.

By practicing healthier thought patterns, we can overcome negative self-talk that leads to distorted self-perceptions and unconstructive responses. I highly recommend visiting the website www.susandavid.com/quiz/ and taking the quiz to assess your emotional agility and learn more about her important work.

The Christian apostle St. Paul understood the importance of replacing negative thoughts with positive thoughts way back in the first century.

> "Finally brothers and sisters, whatever is true,
> whatever is honorable, whatever is just, whatever is pure,
> whatever is lovely, whatever is commendable—
> if there is any moral excellence and if there is
> anything praiseworthy—dwell on these things."
> —PHILIPPIANS 4:8, (Christian Standards Bible)

According to historical records, St. Paul, while imprisoned in either Rome or Ephesus, wrote a letter to the Christian congregation he had founded in Philippi around 62 CE. Despite his situation's grim circumstances, he focused on positivity and urged the Philippians to do the same. He recognized the detrimental impact of dwelling on negative emotions like fear and despair, particularly in the face of his own impending execution. In the letter, he implored the Philippians to prioritize their happiness and find joy in their faith, saying, "I want you to be happy, always happy in the Lord; I repeat, what I want is your happiness."

By recognizing and empathizing with the fragility of others, we are more easily able to project positivity toward them, even as we disagree with or correct them. As we build our own antifragility, we become happier and more confident, which again helps us project more positivity into the world. And then we are on the road to excellence.

CHAPTER 5

Purposeful Leadership

"An organization is only as strong as
its leadership and its people."
—JOHN MAXWELL

NOW THAT YOU HAVE AN UNDERSTANDING OF OUR SHADOW SELVES, of how you can project positivity using the laws of attraction and conformity, of how you can use culture to your advantage, and of how you can be sympathetic to the fragility of others while building your own antifragility, you have a choice to become a more effective leader.

St. Thomas Aquinas believed that one of the most exceptional qualities of human beings is our "dignity of causality." By this, he meant that we possess the ability to exercise free choice and make a difference in the world, thanks to our intellect and will. As causal beings, we have the unique capacity to change direction, rectify our mistakes, and strive to improve ourselves every day.

You can choose to continue managing as if the world has not changed, as if the pandemic has not altered the workforce, and as if the status quo is "good enough."

"If you don't know where you are going,
any road will get you there."
—LEWIS CARROLL

Or you can choose to set a clear goal to increase positivity for yourself and your organization. You can choose to up your game to find your excellence. If this is your choice (and my goal is to convince you it should be!), then you must understand these concepts and purposefully use them—in business or otherwise.

The strength of an organization depends on the mindset and attitude of its people and its leadership. Becoming a better leader involves, in part, increasing your confidence and the confidence of your organization, understanding your impact on others, and being intentional about the way you communicate with your people.

Building Confidence

Effective leadership begins with individual confidence, and individual confidence is the key to organizational confidence. We can't expect our organizations to be confident and flourishing without believing in what we do and having confidence in our jobs. After all, can you imagine working for someone who lacks confidence and perspective and has no vision for a brighter future? Having someone who can guide us on this arduous path called life, including in the workplace, is essential. We must be that person for the others in our organizations.

Our positivity and assurance are the foundation of our leadership. They are the starting point for building team confidence, leading to an optimistic culture and team alignment, which eventually result in organizational excellence. Therefore, a leader's confidence and understanding are necessary for creating a confident environment for everyone else.

> "Repetition leads to confidence.
> Confidence leads to courage."
> —RYAN HOLIDAY

To develop your confidence, you must put in the work and the repetition. When you are competent at your job and prepared for the tasks at hand, you have the confidence to lead and project the shadow of that assurance onto others.

Years ago I read *Nuts!*, a book by Kevin and Jackie Freiberg about Herb Kelleher, the co-founder and CEO of Southwest Airlines. Kelleher was a renowned business leader whose enthusiastic leadership style inspired his team. He believed that taking care of employees leads to happy employees who, in turn, take care of their customers. Kelleher's passion, energy, and exceptional approach to managing his team played a significant role in shaping the culture of Southwest Airlines. His contribution to the airline industry is a testament to the power of putting people first in leadership, as well as to positivity and passion. Today, Southwest Airlines continues to thrive, most likely due to the legacy of leadership culture that Kelleher left behind.

Kelleher was a charismatic leader. He cared about excellence and success for himself and his people. His energy and positivity created massive attraction. His confidence and charisma were the driving force in creating organizational conformity to the Southwest culture. He used love, humor, passion, and brand design to create attraction and buy-in. As he said and believed, "A company is stronger if it is bound by love rather than by fear."

Kelleher's approach to achieving organizational excellence began with his own sense of self. He was the driving force behind the company's success; his positivity and individual confidence served as the catalyst that led to team confidence and trust. This cultural shift paved the way for organizational excellence and positive outcomes for over four decades.

Understanding Our Impact on the World

When you work on becoming a more positive and confident leader, you create a significant ripple effect. Many of us tend to underestimate our incredible impact on the world. We often view ourselves as insignificant individuals with little responsibility toward others. However, in reality, our actions can cause a massive shift in our culture and transform the world for the better (or worse). This truth is captured in a poem by Donna Ashworth, taken from her book *I Wish I Knew*:[6]

---

[6] Reprinted with permission from author.

YOUR BEAUTIFUL PATHWAY

You are trailing a beautiful pathway through this life
an invisible
star-bright network of *you*.
All the times you touch the hearts of others
are stars on that trail.
Every time you smile
give advice
show kindness
stars
all of them.
Your twinkly star-bright galaxy of you
is growing every day
reaching places that you haven't even been to
but your energy has
through your words or your actions.
You are snaking a shimmering pathway
full of love and joy
sincerity and kindness
companionship and loyalty
and you-ness
all over the place
and you don't even see it.
If you could
you would be mesmerized
by the effect you have on this planet.
Keep trailing that beautiful pathway
you have so much more to add.
And one day
others will follow that trail
made by you
Made *just* by *you*.

It is estimated that each of us will come in direct contact with at least eighty thousand people throughout our lives. Every interaction we have with others can create a chain reaction of positive change as they, in turn, pass on our influence to others. This ripple effect has the power to create an extraordinary transformation in our society, affecting the lives of countless people. If we truly grasped the magnitude of our influence, I think we would likely behave more responsibly and act with greater compassion and positivity toward others.

I see this firsthand in my organization. There is a reason why McDonald's signs say "billions and billions served." At one of our locations, we serve up to three thousand people per day. Just one drive-thru order-taker/cashier might interact with 650 carloads of people. That is a lot of opportunity to provide hospitality, or what McDonald's refers to as "golden moments," that can make a difference in the customer's day. I am always fascinated by the number of lives we touch. For example, consider this email I recently received from a customer:

Mr. Abbate:

I drive into the drive-thru every morning at around 5 a.m. I always order the same thing every day. The girl that helps me almost on a daily basis is really nice and she always knows what I want in my coffee. She always is a bright face that I see every morning! Recently, she talked me into downloading the app, and now I get at least 1 free coffee a week. Her name is Misty. She has shown me kindness, and she is a ray of sunshine to me. I want to thank your company for having such friendly people working for you!

The fact that the customer was impressed enough to take the time to thank us for her experience goes a long way toward demonstrating the power of our reach and how big our lives can be if we so choose. Misty touches more than six hundred lives a day through our drive-thru. She is impacting the world, one customer at a time! Not too bad for someone whom society likes to disparage as having nothing more than a "McJob."

> "If you work just for money, you'll never make it,
> but if you love what you're doing and you always put
> the customer first, success will be yours."
> —RAY KROC

Digital versus Face-to-Face Communication

As you begin intentionally projecting positivity and confidence to ultimately reach organizational excellence, be intentional about the way you communicate with your people as well. Social media interaction is powerful and influential, but face-to-face human interactions have the most impact, as shown by a recent study conducted during the lockdown period and published on Nature.com.[7]

This study confirmed that the multitude of digital communication tools and services available today differs significantly from face-to-face interaction. Though digital communication is convenient, it lacks critical nonverbal cues that face-to-face communication

---

[7] Maximilian Monninger et al., "Real-Time Individual Benefit from Social Interactions before and during the Lockdown: The Crucial Role of Personality, Neurobiology and Genes," *Translational Psychiatry* 12 (2022): 28, https://doi.org/10.1038/s41398-022-01799-z.

offers, such as body language, facial expressions, and tone of voice. In-person conversations help us form deeper connections and better understand each other, which is crucial for mental well-being. When texting, emailing, or video calling, it's easy to miss essential communication elements, and this causes misunderstandings and misinterpretations, making it hard to connect emotionally and creating distance between people.

During a recent conversation with one of my supervisors, he made a surprising admission. He revealed that, for a long time, he avoided using the gallery feature on Zoom during video calls because it made him nervous. He explained that seeing only my face on the screen made him focus too much on my facial expressions and how they might indicate my perception of the meeting content. Interestingly, he was not nervous during in-person meetings. This revelation was unexpected, but it aligns with the data and sheds light on the nuances of communication in virtual environments.

Ideally, to build relationships with the people in your organization, you will find ways to communicate with them in person, at least periodically. Realistically, however, with the recent prevalence of remote work, you will often have to rely on digital communication. In this case, you should at least be aware of its limitations and find ways to make up for them.

A famous 1989 United Airlines commercial demonstrates one way to overcome reliance on digital communication in the workplace.[8] Produced by the brilliant advertising firm Leo Burnett, also the lead advertising firm for McDonald's at the time, the

---

[8] Leo Burnett USA, "7L: United Airlines Commercial 1990 'Speech,'" August 16, 2010, YouTube video, 1:00, https://youtu.be/mU2rpcAABbA.

commercial highlights the universality of communication problems and the necessity of face-to-face conversations. It features Ben, the CEO of a company that was just fired by a longstanding and highly valued client. Ben convenes a quick management meeting, looking haggard and distraught, to announce the news that the company is losing touch with its clients and needs to reinvigorate its relationships with them (in two hundred-plus cities). An assistant hands Ben a stack of United tickets, and Ben begins handing them out to the individual managers, who look stunned and confused. As Ben leaves the room, someone asks him where he's going. He replies, "To visit that old friend who fired us this morning."

The message conveyed in the commercial is that people should not solely rely on email, text, Zoom, or cell phones to stay in touch with others. Social media should not be the only means to maintain relationships. We must remember that human beings thrive in community with other human beings. The better you nurture and strengthen that sense of community, the better your leadership will be.

CHAPTER 6

Beauty

"Beauty is not in the face; beauty
is a light in the heart."
—KAHLIL GIBRAN

I've discussed how understanding the shadows we cast and becoming more confident, purposeful leaders puts us on the road to excellence, and I've argued that one of the challenges to achieving excellence is that society is becoming increasingly divided, fragile, and dysfunctional. In this chapter, I want to propose an ancient solution to this modern problem: lead with beauty. Beauty is the first of the transcendental (nonphysical) virtues referred to in the introduction of this book.

Plato, a renowned philosopher from more than two thousand years ago, believed that three essential transcendental virtues can aid humans in achieving excellence and contentment: beauty, truth, and goodness. He believed beauty and attraction transcend the physical, that beauty is an expression of goodness and truth. These virtues are not just abstract concepts; they hold significant importance in our daily lives. In today's increasingly complex and fragile world, we can seek comfort and guidance in the ancient wisdom of these virtues as well as in the divine narrative of the Bible.[9]

The concept of transcendental virtues is both fascinating and profound. It refers to a realm that exists beyond our everyday experiences—a nonphysical, immaterial, conceptual, or even spiritual sphere. In philosophy, the transcendental realm seeks to explain the nature of reality and being. The virtues of beauty, truth, and goodness are timeless universal attributes of being that help us understand the world and our place in it. When we come across organizations, relationships, and creative works that embody these virtues, we experience a sense of completeness and peace that takes us to a higher place. Essentially, we find contentment and some element of excellence.

Certain things in this world possess an evident beauty that not only attracts us but also opens the door to the possibility of experiencing truth and goodness. For instance, seeing a beautiful waterfall or majestic tree can evoke feelings of attraction and gratitude while potentially leading us to discover more about life and its goodness. A beautiful math equation can attract us while leading us to deeper truths and greater goodness. The beauty of music or a church can also profoundly impact our senses, emotions, and spiritual well-being. On the other hand, a beautiful pair of shoes offers only a temporary attraction with no specific goodness attached to it. Similarly, the physical beauty of a person may evoke attraction and admiration, but the person's physical beauty may not lead to discovering truth or the greater goodness in the world that leads to contentment.

---

[9] Kenneth Samples, "The 3 Transcendentals: Truth, Goodness, & Beauty," Reasons to Believe, February 2, 2021, https://reasons.org/explore/blogs/reflections/the-3 -transcendentals-truth-goodness-beauty.

St. Augustine's *Confessions* contains a profound statement that touches the very core of our being. The Christian bishop and theologian writes, "You have made us for yourself, O Lord, and our hearts are restless until they rest in You." This statement encapsulates humanity's innermost longings. The restlessness we feel is an unending quest for fulfillment and satisfaction that can be found only in divine beauty, truth, and goodness.

Are you or others you love experiencing this same restlessness? Are you searching for something more? Are social media and superficial relationships ultimately leaving you empty? Maybe it is time to look deeper into biblical wisdom to discover true beauty.

Biblical Wisdom

"But the Lord said to Samuel, 'Do not look on his appearance or on the height of his stature, because I have rejected him. For the Lord sees not as man sees; man looks on the outward appearance, but the Lord looks on the heart.'"

—1 SAMUEL 16:7 (Revised Standard Version)

This verse is part of the story in the Bible where God instructs the prophet Samuel to anoint a new king of Israel, as King Saul has been rejected by God for his disobedience. Samuel visits Jesse's house to find the chosen king among Jesse's sons.

The significance of this Scripture verse lies in the contrast between human judgment and God's perspective. Upon seeing Jesse's eldest son, Eliab, Samuel is inclined to think he should be king because of his impressive appearance and stature. However, God rebukes Samuel not to rely on external appearances when making the decision. God instead selects David, the youngest son of Jesse, despite his young age, appearance, and background as a lowly shepherd. This story highlights the precedence of inner qualities over outward appearances. It reminds me of the old saying "You can't judge a book by its cover."

The lesson of this biblical narrative bodes well for us today. It emphasizes that God looks beyond outward appearances and instead assesses a person's character and inner qualities. In choosing a king, God is more interested in the sons' integrity, faith, and devotion than their physical attributes or worldly accomplishments. While the human tendency is to make snap judgments about others based on appearance or other superficial criteria, God has his own criteria for selecting individuals for specific roles—and these are not limited by human conventions or expectations. Because our judgments can be shallow and flawed, God reminds us in this verse to adopt a more discerning perspective.

> "Your beauty should not come from outward adornment, such as elaborate hairstyles and the wearing of gold jewelry or fine clothes. Rather, it should be that of your inner self, the unfading beauty of a gentle and quiet spirit, which is of great worth in God's sight."
> —1 PETER 3:3–4 (New International Version)

In this teaching, Peter guides Christian women on the significance of their attire and beauty. He emphasizes that true worth in the eyes of God is not determined by external beauty or physical appearance but rather by the inner qualities of a person. Peter encourages women to prioritize cultivating a "gentle and quiet spirit," which is the radiance of beauty. This verse serves as a reminder of the transcendental virtues associated with inner beauty, kindness, and humility, as opposed to superficial or external attributes. It emphasizes that these inner qualities are enduring and invaluable in the sight of God and contribute to a person's contentment and fulfillment.

> "Charm is deceptive, and beauty is fleeting,
> but a woman who fears the *Lord* is to be praised."
> —PROVERBS 31:30 (New International Version)

In this verse, the word *fear* does not refer to a negative sense of dread, as it does today, but instead implies having a deep respect and appreciation for God's wisdom and word. Proverbs, a book found in the Old Testament, is a treasure trove of wise sayings attributed mainly to King Solomon. It comprises a collection of concise statements that offer direction on moral conduct, practical living, and human nature's insights.

Defining True Beauty

> "Beauty is the radiance of truth and the
> fragrance of goodness."
> —FATHER VINCENT MCNABB, OP

We as a society have a warped sense of beauty. Understanding the true meaning of beauty is crucial to avoid falling prey to superficial aspects that don't truly matter; beauty is not only an expression of form. St. Thomas Aquinas, a doctor of the Church and one of the greatest thinkers in our history, describes beauty in the following manner: "Integrity or perfection, since those things which are impaired are by the very fact ugly; Due proportion or harmony; and lastly, brightness, or clarity, whence things are called beautiful which have a bright color" (Summa Theologica I q. 39. art 8). In other words, beauty encompasses all that is good, pure, and true.

To change our secular perception, we begin by journeying into the fascinating world of beauty, where misconceptions and misrepresentations often prevail to our peril. The original etymology of *beauty* can be derived from the Latin words *bene* (adv.), meaning "well, in the right way, honorably, properly"; *bellus*, meaning "handsome, fine, pretty"; *beatus*, meaning "blessed"; and *beare*, meaning "to make blessed."

Plato's idea of beauty is not a physical attribute but a profound concept encompassing truth, honor, and goodness. However, in our current culture, we have an obsession with beauty in its most literal definition, often reinforced by social media or consumerism. This sophomoric definition, which is a deviation from Plato's original vision, can lead to feelings of inadequacy and unworthiness for many people. Shifting our perspective and embracing the deeper meaning of beauty, far beyond superficial appearance, is crucial for our well-being.

We often describe babies as beautiful and feel drawn to their innocence, purity, and truth. What is it about them that we find so beautiful? Their inherent goodness and truthfulness captivate us. But we also use *beautiful* to describe cars, fashion models, and other objects. Why do we do this? At first glance, a baby and these things aren't comparable. However, an underlying attraction draws us in. We must stop equating beauty with superficial appearances and start looking for beauty in the things that truly matter. The truth is that beauty takes many forms that transcend the physical.

I have described the significance of the law of attraction and how it shapes our lives. Our thoughts and focus determine our reality, so if we focus on positivity and beauty, we attract more positivity and beauty into our lives. However, attraction depends on our perception of beauty. If we have a distorted view of beauty, truth, and goodness, our perception is affected and the law of attraction does not work as well. For instance, if we define beauty as having pleasing physical attributes, we might not see the beauty within us and, as a result, limit ourselves from achieving our true potential.

As a society, we have been conditioned to place importance on physical appearance. We are constantly bombarded with (usually digitally enhanced) images of flawless skin, perfect hair, and toned bodies. This narrow perspective has a significant negative impact on our confidence and self-worth. Let's face it: none of us has flawless skin, perfect hair, and a perfectly toned body.

When we prioritize superficial beauty, we are essentially setting ourselves up for failure because physical appearance is constantly changing and fleeting. Take a moment to compare how someone looks at eighty versus how they looked at twenty. Too much emphasis on physical beauty can lead to a sense of doom, as it is not something that can be sustained in the long term.

Furthermore, relying on physical beauty as the foundation of our identity or self-worth is not a sustainable approach to long-term contentment. The most beautiful people in the world are often the most insecure about their physical beauty, maybe because they are their own worst critics, or maybe because they "put all their eggs in one basket," as the saying goes. In other words, they have attached their self-worth to the most fleeting and temporal aspect of their humanity! We are much more than just our physical appearances; limiting ourselves to this narrow perspective hinders our personal growth and prevents us from reaching our full potential.

It's no secret that attraction plays a significant role in our lives. The law of attraction is fundamental to who we are, and beauty is an essential factor contributing to it. While we tend to be drawn to physical beauty, it's not the defining factor of attraction.

Beauty can be found in other unique qualities, such as symmetry, grace, confidence, orderliness, radiance, inspiration, purpose, and creativity. Beauty captivates, inspires, and persuades others. It's an undeniable truth that we must live with beauty in our lives to attract good things. However, we should strive to define beauty beyond physical appearance and focus on the unique qualities that make us attractive.

Finding Your Beauty

"To be beautiful means to be yourself.
You don't need to be accepted by others.
You need to accept yourself."
—THICH NHAT HANH, *The Art of Power*

For leaders, recognizing and appreciating both external and inner beauty is crucial. Leaders who possess kindness, empathy, and compassion naturally attract the same, which leads to organizational beauty. But if you fail to recognize the importance of beauty and neglect to cultivate it within your team, your organization may struggle to thrive. Therefore, taking time to reflect on your leadership style and how it aligns with the concept of beauty is essential. If you can embrace and harness your unique beauty, you can effortlessly inspire and guide your team toward achieving a beautiful and excellent organization. To attract others to ourselves, we must lead with our beauty. To attract others to our mission, we must leverage our mission's beauty!

Finding your beauty is intrinsically linked to your self-confidence, which is vital for achieving excellence and finding contentment. We have all struggled with self-confidence before, at times feeling inadequate for the task at hand. For example, I have always been passionate about sports—specifically basketball—but being only five foot eight inches tall limited my potential success. I experienced signs of baldness in my early twenties, which impacted my confidence. I also struggled with shyness when I was young, which made tasks like public speaking difficult for me. I learned that to build self-confidence in the face of these challenges, I had to focus on the things I could control and let go of those I could not.

To find your beauty and thus build self-confidence, begin honing the areas of your life in which you feel good about yourself, whether your work, physical appearance, hobbies, or relationships. Look for things that provide you with positivity and some sense of accomplishment. Take little steps consistently over time and you will pave the way for significant progress in your life.

In my case, though I wasn't tall enough to truly excel in basketball, I could achieve excellent physical fitness—so I've made consistent exercise and proper nutrition part of my daily routine for more than four decades. Two of my strengths are curiosity and the love of learning, so I focused on education and reading to enhance my growth and my knowledge base. I worked on my communication skills and practiced public speaking regularly to overcome my shyness. Rather than dwelling on my perceived or actual weaknesses, I chose to leverage my strengths and work to find progress in areas I could control. Over time, this led to a significant improvement in my self-confidence. I believe the virtue of temperance allowed me to be disciplined enough to accomplish these things. Ryan Holiday sums it up in his book *Discipline Is Destiny*: "No one has a harder time than the lazy. No one experiences more pain than the glutton. No success is shorter lived than the reckless or endlessly ambitious. Failing to realize your full potential is a terrible punishment. Greed moves the goalposts, preventing one from ever enjoying what one has. Even if the outside world celebrates them, on the inside there is only misery, self-loathing, and dependence."

The process of continuous improvement involves setting goals, taking action, gathering feedback, and making adjustments based on that feedback. It is a self-improvement feedback loop that allows for exponential growth. This strategy has enabled me to experience significant personal growth and development—people are often surprised to learn that I identify as an introvert and used to fear public speaking because of shyness. The strategy can be a powerful tool for anyone looking to enhance self-confidence and achieve goals.

In today's world, where the media often criticize less-than-perfect bodies and perpetuate unrealistic beauty standards, we must take a step back and reflect on how we define and perceive our beauty. We need to find a better way to overcome societal norms in order to move forward as leaders in our families, businesses, and communities. We must reeducate ourselves and others on what it truly means to be beautiful human beings made in the image and likeness of our Creator.

By consciously recognizing, embracing, and celebrating beauty in all its diverse forms, we not only find excellence in our organizations, but we also work toward creating a world that is more accepting, harmonious, and inclusive of everyone's unique qualities.

Beauty in Business

The concept of beauty is important in our work environments as well. If I want a McDonald's restaurant to be exceptional, I must begin with beauty. If I want a product to be successful, the designer must begin with some characteristics of beauty.

> "It requires a certain kind of mind to see beauty
> in a hamburger bun. Yet is it any more unusual to find grace
> in the texture and softly carved silhouette of a bun than
> to reflect lovingly on the hackles of a fishing fly?
> Or the arrangements and textures on a butterfly's wing?
> Not if you are a McDonald's man."
> —RAY KROC

In the context of McDonald's, beauty comes from striving for excellence, providing radiant hospitality, maintaining clean and organized restaurants, having confident and competent leadership, showing passion for the brand, and promoting order and symmetry over chaos and dysfunction. We must radiate beauty through these characteristics to attract customers and good employees to our restaurants.

Imagine walking into a restaurant that is untidy and dirty, with a staff that seems frazzled as they run a chaotic kitchen. Would you consider the restaurant beautiful and attractive? Unlikely. The same goes for any organization. It won't attract anyone if it's messy, dysfunctional, negative, pessimistic, dirty, and unprofessional. That kind of environment, according to the law of attraction, will not lead to the beauty that attracts the right people who will elevate the organization.

When hiring, we need to think about beauty—not the physical beauty revered by our secular culture, but the deeper, more nuanced beauty of our ancient past. Does the candidate possess the qualities that represent the brand image? At McDonald's, this could be a welcoming smile, an orderly appearance, and a positive attitude. Then, once a candidate is hired, we must do our part to support the new hire by executing an orientation program and training plan that reinforces the concept of beautiful hospitality.

In the following excerpt from an interview with Jonathon, a supervisor of several McDonald's restaurants in California, he describes what he sees as beauty in restaurants.

> The first thing I would say is that it starts with the employees. Are they happy? That's the number one thing. I've been in several small mom and pop restaurants where the employees look miserable. They're just existing. But you go to other places and the employees are happy. You can tell whether employees are happy or not based on body language, eye contact, and so forth.
>
> The other thing would be cleanliness. I don't know if it's just the McDonald's operator in me, but when I go to restaurants, I'm looking at dust in the vents and lighting, dirt in the bathroom corners —everything.

Culture plays a big role, too. When I go into Starbucks, I see an employee board displaying a customer of the month, employee of the month, and their favorite drinks. Their employees look genuinely happy. In one of my restaurants, one of my GMs does something like that, but she does it with graduations in school. If an employee does well in high school or college, she has a board that congratulates them publicly, and the employees genuinely love it. You can't develop and you can't have excellence if employees don't like coming to work. The culture has to be beautiful.

The design of the original McDonald's restaurants is a good illustration of how physical beauty helps the success of a business. Back in 1952, the McDonald brothers, Dick and Mac, collaborated with the gifted Los Angeles architect Stanley Clark Meston to create a unique and innovative roadside restaurant design for McDonald's. They hoped to create a beautiful, futuristic design in anticipation of franchising their restaurant concept. During their brainstorming sessions, Dick presented his idea of incorporating two half circles at either end of the structure to capture the attention of passing motorists. Meston, who had previously worked as a set designer for Universal Studios, transformed Dick's half circles into a pair of stunning twenty-five-foot-high tapered structures illuminated with neon lights. The design embraced the newly emerging architectural style of neo-futurism, which had gained popularity during that period. The incorporation of these elements into the building's construction was a defining feature and created an instant attraction. Meston's design made its debut in 1953 with the first franchised McDonald's in Phoenix, Arizona. You can see it in the photo of the third McDonald's built with Meston's design, which still stands today in Downey, California.[10]

The first McDonald's franchise that my father managed was built in 1969 and was one of the very last buildings of this style.

Over the past fifty years, McDonald's has had many iterations of architectural designs, like the latest style, shown in the following image, and all have been about creating a sense of beauty. We want our physical exterior to project an image that has the potential to attract customers and present the brand as innovative and modern.

---

[10] Jonathan Glancey, "The Strange Story of the World's Most Famous Logo," BBC, November 6, 2017, https://www.bbc.com/culture/article/20160830-mcdonalds -golden-arches-the-strange-story-of-an-icon.

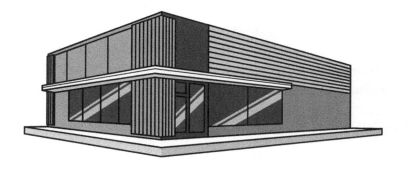

As an owner of McDonald's restaurants, I can attest that this business requires a significant investment. Our capital is frequently reinvested into the physical plant of the restaurant, as we are required, per our franchise agreement, to conduct a major interior overhaul every ten years and a massive rebuild or significant exterior reimaging every twenty to twenty-five years. The expenses for these types of investments can be in the millions and can be challenging to accept, particularly if the restaurant is only marginally profitable. However, because we are all part of a greater brand, maintaining consistency and appearance is crucial.

I have executed numerous rebuilds, relocations, and significant remodels in my career. Throughout my ventures, I have noticed a consistent pattern regarding the impact that extensive exterior reimaging has on sales. A well-designed, modern, and visually appealing restaurant has a magnetic effect on customers. Upon completion of such projects, I have observed a remarkable increase in sales, ranging from 15 percent to 30 percent. The restaurant's new look and feel acts as a beacon of attraction, enticing lost customers to give us another try and drawing in customers from our competitors.

Furthermore, it encourages existing customers to visit more often, ultimately increasing our customer retention rate.

Another benefit of rebranding is that it enhances the employee experience, which translates into improved customer service. When the environment is clean, modern, and attractive, it creates a positive and welcoming work atmosphere for employees. They feel happier and more hospitable, which is then reflected in their interactions with customers.

Of course, once we have attracted more customers, to maintain them as customers we must also deliver on our brand promise. However, the restaurant's revamped aesthetics is the attraction we need to reset the environment and provide the opportunity to deliver on our brand's truth and goodness.

CHAPTER 7

Truth

"There is nothing more beautiful than your authentic truth."
—THE RED FAIRY PROJECT

BEAUTY, WHILE CAPTIVATING, EVENTUALLY LEAVES US YEARNING FOR something more enduring and consequential than mere sensory appeal. We all crave truth, the second of the three essential transcendental virtues. Defining and living our truth is the next step on the road to excellence.

Beauty alone, be it in the form of a well-maintained house, a neatly dressed individual, a pleasant demeanor, or physical attractiveness, is enticing but insufficient over time. To establish lasting relationships, we require a deeper, more authentic, and truthful connection. Even if someone possesses physical charm, without depth and the ability to convey truth, that person tends to have faltering relationships. We all seek connections that transcend superficial attraction. Beauty may serve as a magnet, but for relationships to stand the test of time, truth must be the anchor.

Truth plays a vital role in our lives. It is rational, logical, and unwavering, offering us a sense of security, confidence, and stability.

When we are drawn to someone or something, it is wise to make sure that person or thing embodies these qualities. Otherwise, we risk finding ourselves entangled in unsatisfying jobs and relationships and making poor decisions. The law of attraction may suggest that beauty is the initial magnet, but in the end, the enduring truth is what truly captivates us and keeps us grounded in our commitments.

Truth in Ancient Greece

The concept of truth can be traced back to the ancient Greek word *logos*. In ancient Greek culture, this term had several meanings and interpretations depending on the context in which it was used.

For example, logos was connected to the idea of making persuasive arguments based on reason and evidence, and it played a crucial role in the development of logical reasoning. This aspect of logos was particularly important in the works of philosophers like Plato and Aristotle.

Logos could also refer to the concept of proportion and ratio. This mathematical aspect of logos was used in various geometric and mathematical discussions.

Similarly, some ancient Greek thinkers, such as Pythagoras and the Pythagoreans, associated logos with the belief in a cosmic harmony or order that could be expressed through mathematical relationships and ratios.

Truth and Christianity

In Christian tradition, the term *logos*, or *truth*, takes on a theological and philosophical meaning. The concept of the logos in

Christian theology is closely associated with the nature and role of Jesus Christ and is used as a title for him.

The Gospel of John opens with a declaration that "in the beginning was the Word, and the Word was with God, and the Word was God" (John 1:1). The term *Word* here is derived from the Greek word *logos*. This passage is often interpreted as meaning that Jesus Christ, as the Logos, is the incarnate Word of God, existing from the beginning and having a divine nature.

The Logos is believed to be the divine agent through whom God created the universe. The idea of the Logos influences this concept as the rational and creative principle, and it is expressed in the Christian doctrine of creation.

The Logos, in the person of Jesus Christ, is seen as the redeemer and savior of humanity. Through his life, death, and resurrection, Jesus Christ is believed to have reconciled humanity with God and offered salvation.

The Logos is a crucial concept in Christian theology that explains Christ's divinity and the trinitarian doctrine. It played a significant role in early Christian debates and the formation of creeds, such as the Nicene Creed. The Logos connects the ancient philosophical and theological traditions to the Christian faith, making it an essential and distinctive part of Christian theology.[11]

---

[11] "Logos," PBS: Faith and Reason, accessed August 14, 2024, https://www.pbs.org/faithandreason/theogloss/logos-body.html.

> "We are building a dictatorship of relativism that does
> not recognize anything as definitive and whose ultimate
> goal consists solely of one's own ego and desires."
> —POPE BENEDICT XVI

Some people adhere to moral relativism, the belief that people can choose their own truths based on convenience or personal objectives. But there are some natural and culturally established truths that form the foundation of a community and society. These truths are essential for creating a cohesive and supportive culture.

Unfortunately, throughout history, people have been misled into embracing political, moral, and social ideals of freedom that never really deliver. Resisting being misled in this way is especially important when living our faith within our families and communities because we are all interconnected. One person's idea of freedom can have a profound effect on another person's freedom. Ultimately, we are all sojourners on a journey toward true freedom, regardless of our religious beliefs. Our understanding of freedom must be directed toward the truth of who we are, deep in our souls. Therefore, we should always strive to be there for each other and live in reasoned and ordered communion with each other; that is the only way human freedom can exist.

Finding Your Truth

Throughout the last two decades, I have embarked on numerous religious pilgrimages in search of my own truth and to support its development. These experiences have been invaluable in helping me stay aligned with the truth I strive for versus society's truth.

Although most of us know deep down the kind of life we should lead, it's easy to stray from our North Star. Just discovering our truth is not enough; living it and executing it is a daily battle for each one of us. As flawed and compromised creatures, we are easily manipulated from our truth due to the laws of attraction and conformity.

For example, consider the infamous corporation Enron. The Enron scandal is widely regarded as one of the most notorious corporate scandals in history. The controversy began in early 2001 when experts raised questions about the accounts presented in the company's annual report for the previous year. Enron's accountants had adopted various nonstandard procedures, which made discerning the company's actual financial standing difficult. Having a presence in energy, commodities, and telecoms, Enron and its revenue was a mystery to most analysts. Soon, the Securities and Exchange Commission initiated an investigation and unearthed the fact that Enron had concealed billions of dollars in liabilities through companies it controlled, which made it appear profitable even when it was incurring losses. As the crisis unfolded, Enron's stock price plummeted from $90.56 to less than one dollar, forcing the company to file for what was then the largest Chapter 11 bankruptcy in history. The company's employees lost billions in stock value, and several of its top executives ended up in prison.[12]

For a while, Enron looked beautiful, but ultimately, it was unable to deliver truth. Its executives may have started with good intentions, but they strayed further and further from truth, thereby causing harm to themselves and others.

---

[12] Adam Hayes, "What Was Enron? What Happened and Who Was Responsible," Investopedia, last modified March 1, 2024, https://www.investopedia.com/terms/e/enron.asp.

As humans, we are all tempted to stray from the truth, either intentionally, to make our lives easier in some way, or unintentionally, due to the influence of pervasive nontruths that surround us. That's why it's crucial to have a process in place that helps you stay aligned with your truth once you find it. This could be following a defined religious construct, embracing the values in your workplace, or simply relying on a partner who can hold you accountable to living your truth.

For leaders, finding their truth is quite important. Just as individual beauty leads to organizational beauty, individual truth leads to organizational truth. As Enron showed, the opposite is also true. If you can find your truth and stay aligned with it, your organization will reflect truth as well, attracting customers and employees.

The following excerpt from an interview with Jerry, the director of operations for a McDonald's owner/operator in the Southeast Region of the United States, gives insight into how he leads through his truth, which is his commitment to his people.

> I have been with McDonald's for thirty-nine years now. I describe my job as similar to that of a head coach. As the leader of the team, it's my responsibility to motivate them and provide direction every day. Planning and setting day-to-day goals play a crucial role in my job. Most of my day is spent trying to plan what the team does and give them guidance on what needs to be done.
>
> Early on, I learned that treating people well and gaining their respect was something I needed to do because respect is not given to you. You have to earn the respect of your people. Like my dad—he was a major in the Army. As Provost Marshall, he was in charge of a group of guys. I'd hear him talking about them sometimes. Each

guy had his place and role. Each was good in certain positions. And he led them.

It was the same with McDonald's. I asked myself, can I become the leader of these people? Could I be in control of the grill area? They were my team, back there in the kitchen. Someone would call back to them with a request, a replacement sandwich or correction to an order, and everyone would do their part to make it all come together.

When I was a general manager, I was out in the lobby one day, talking to the customers like I did every day. There were a couple of guys sitting in one of the booths. "What's your name again?" they asked. I told them.

"I told you that was him!" one guy said to the other excitedly.

"What are you talking about?" I said.

They both grinned. "Your dad was our company commander. We were Green Berets. Special Forces, out on the front lines in Vietnam. He got us out of a lot of trouble." They went on to say what he did for them. How much they loved him for what he did. "He was tough," they said, "but he always took care of us."

I always wanted to be that kind of leader. My dad never talked about what he did for his people. Taking care of them was just something he was supposed to do. It wasn't something to brag about. I didn't even know he was a Green Beret until these men told me.

That's our job as leaders, to make sure we take care of our people. If we do, they'll take care of us. In turn, accomplishing the job we're trying to do will come easier for everyone because we're a solid team. You've got their backs, and they have yours. I've always tried to be that person with my people too. We've got a job to do, and I'm glad they're all behind me.

We do more than just sell hamburgers and fries; we manage and help people too. Our assistance extends beyond the restaurant. If anyone asks for my help, I do my best to provide it, whether I'm at another restaurant or at church. For example, if someone wants advice on helping their kid find a job, I always suggest McDonald's. Whenever I can offer a solution and the person values my opinion, I feel good about helping. Ultimately, I believe that helping others is what we're here for.

The following interview with Suki, director of operations for a large McDonald's franchisee in California, demonstrates leadership in action. Suki describes how she leads through her truths, some of which are respect, communication, and appreciation.

My core leadership value is respect. You should treat people the way you want to be treated. No matter what class people are from or what qualifications they may have, you treat them with respect. You don't know their backgrounds. Don't judge them. Give them respect.

I had a crew person who worked the front counter, a . . . guy who had a tough life. He began looking very sad when he came to work. One day, I sat down with him. "I respect your privacy," I said. "If you don't want to share anything, that's fine. But I noticed that you're not who you used to be. Again, I don't want to get into your personal life, but is there anything I can help you with?" All of a sudden, he started to cry and share his story with me. He had to come to work because he needed the money, but he was going through certain stuff and just couldn't deal with customers. He needed his own space. I moved him back to the grill but I respected his privacy as to why I was moving him. I announced, "Starting today, Jose will not be on the front counter. He needs to learn the kitchen." I was able to respect his need to not face customers and to still be able to work whatever hours he wanted. Jose respected me so much more after that. "My own mother wouldn't have done that for me," he said. That just hit my heart. Thank God I was able to recognize him.

Communication is another one of my values. It is the key to success. Whether you're driving a big or small company, or doing something else in your personal life, if you don't communicate with your team properly, you're not going to get results. Right now, I have eight supervisors working under me. I have to make sure my team knows what's going on in the company. I have a method and the method is this: do whatever it takes. I communicate with my team on daily activities and numbers. I work with a lot of different personalities, so I learn how to communicate with each individual. Some are good with email, some with text or phone calls. You can't communicate with everyone the same way. You need different approaches to get through to them. So communicate the way each person will respond to the most. Because at the end of the day, if you communicate properly, you get better results.

Communication goes both ways. They can come to me too. I have an open door. I tell them very straightforwardly, "If you feel I was a little hard on you, talk to me. Sometimes I feel like I'm okay, but I'm a little loud and I don't want people to assume I'm yelling or screaming. That's just who I am." I make sure they know I'm always open to ideas or even to hearing they felt I was a little too strict with them. I always tell my team, "Feedback hurts but it makes you strong."

I also think appreciation is critical. We all feel we work hard, but you gotta recognize the team or individuals when you see they're doing a great job. Recognition doesn't always have to be money. Part of my job is to go in there and make sure I say hello to everyone on the floor that's working. You have to stop and say, "Thank you for doing a great job today," or, "Thank you for showing up to work today even though it's a holiday." I personally go to the restaurants on holidays with gift cards or donuts or fruit to thank and support the employees who showed up to work. I want to show them our goal is the same: let's deliver. They need to know how much we appreciate them keeping the doors open for us on the holidays. They appreciate hearing, "Have a great day with your family!" after work too.

Your Corporate Truth

To help you understand what truth looks like at the corporate level, let's examine truth in the context of McDonald's. Our truth lies in consistency through brand standards, repeatable training, and execution systems. It is the consistent execution of these principles that leads us beyond chaos and toward order, security, job stability, and reliance on our team. By being part of something bigger than ourselves, we align with the truth that we seek.

You might not have heard of Fred Turner, but chances are you have experienced his genius if you have ever visited or worked at a McDonald's restaurant. Fred L. Turner (January 6, 1933–January 7, 2013) was a key figure in the history of McDonald's. He was one of the early pioneers of the company and played a significant role in its growth and success. Fred joined McDonald's in 1956 when it was a small and relatively new fast-food chain. He worked closely with Ray Kroc and helped to build the brand into the global company you see today. He held various positions within the company, including overseeing operations and training. Under his leadership,

McDonald's developed its distinctive training programs, operational systems, and quality standards, which are still used today.

Fred served as the CEO of McDonald's from 1974 to 1987 and as chairman from 1987 to 1990. He was instrumental in making McDonald's a household name around the world and ensuring the consistency of the brand across all locations. His contributions were pivotal in shaping McDonald's into the international fast-food giant it is today. He was known for his commitment to quality, service, and cleanliness, principles that continue to be at the core of McDonald's operations. Turner passed away in 2013, leaving behind a lasting legacy for me and millions of others.

Fred established the truth of the McDonald's brand. He was maniacal in his focus and commitment to setting standards and developing tools for employees to execute those standards consistently. He accomplished this in two distinct ways: by creating the original operations manual and by founding Hamburger University.

The operations manual, often called the QSC&V (quality, service, cleanliness, and value) manual, is a comprehensive guide outlining the standardized procedures and practices that all McDonald's restaurants worldwide should follow. It covers everything from food preparation and service standards to restaurant cleanliness and customer service. This manual has been fundamental in ensuring consistency and quality across McDonald's locations globally. In the last fifty-plus years, if you were to go into any McDonald's, you would almost certainly find a small version of the QSC&V manual tucked into the general manager's back pocket. Before the digital age made a paper manual obsolete, the manual was a visible sign that the general manager was committed to upholding the brand's truth!

Fred founded Hamburger University (HU) in 1961 to train and educate McDonald's employees, from crew members to senior managers. It offers various programs and courses to develop the skills and knowledge needed to run a McDonald's restaurant and covers restaurant operations, leadership, management, and more. The program has become a cornerstone of McDonald's training and development efforts, contributing to the standardization and quality control that are integral to the McDonald's brand.

I attended HU more than thirty years ago. It was a two-week class back then. Future McDonald's leaders had to take a series of classes for two to three years before they could apply to HU. To be accepted, they had to pass an HU entrance exam. Then, in the two weeks they attended HU, they had to pass a series of tests to ensure they had the knowledge and ability to run a McDonald's restaurant. If they passed all the tests, they received a diploma. Today, the process has been streamlined and modified to allow for greater access and success for a new generation of McDonald's general managers. However, the legacy of Fred and his vision remains through the HU experience.

To learn more about the history and truth of McDonald's, I highly recommend reading *Grinding It Out* by Ray Kroc or *McDonald's: Behind the Arches* by John F. Love. Both of these books highlight the genius and overarching impact of Fred Turner on the McDonald's success story. I had the chance to work with him on a project called the Turner Toast Test in the mid-1990s. He was retired by then and living in Hawaii. However, he came out of retirement with a vengeance to lead McDonald's back to a renewed focus on the quality of products and operations. He was committed to the McDonald's brand truth until the day he passed away.

When Truths Misalign

Your personal and family life can only thrive if your truth is authentic and aligned with your values. Similarly, if you do not believe in your organization's mission and your truth is not aligned with the work you do, you will never be able to flourish within it. To succeed, you must have a foundational truth that matches your organization's values.

Sometimes, the values and beliefs of an organization may not align with the truth you believe or seek. This can create a situation where the organizational principles differ from what you expect. If you are to be remarkable in your organization, your truth must be consistent with the organization's truth. As a leader, I try to communicate the "why" in organizational decisions. I want everyone to understand the logic behind our decisions. When employees understand the "why," I find greater acceptance and ability to implement.

I have to admit that McDonald's needs help with the implementation of consistent organizational truth. To give one example, we struggle to enforce the rule to come to work with a professional appearance. The appearance standards at McDonald's have drastically changed over the past few decades. For most of the last forty years, there has been a basic understanding of professional appearance standards, and yet, over the past three years, we have struggled to find common ground. Every day, I see wrinkled shirts not correctly washed, unshaved faces, unkept hair, pants worn without belts, and the wrong type of shoes. Given the inconsistency with which employees show up to work, our managers are hesitant to send people home for not following the dress code.

During COVID-19, we were happy just to have a workforce; thus, standards across the board were overlooked or eliminated. People would just as soon wear a face mask as shave! Yet we are in the hospitality business, and it's difficult to provide a "golden moment" from behind a mask.

Our challenge as leaders is to communicate the "why" of our truth. Ultimately, if an employee chooses not to accept the "why," then we must both choose a different path.

Using Setbacks to Find Truth

"The road to success is always
under construction."
—RAY KROC

Sometimes setbacks in whatever you are endeavoring to do help you reevaluate and discover a different, better path. The story of how my brother and I became owner/operators of our own franchise stores is an excellent example.

My family's journey as part of the McDonald's franchise system has been an incredible experience. Initially, my brother and I worked alongside our father and learned the ropes of the business under his guidance. He was a great leader and mentor who taught us everything we needed to know in those early days. He was authentic and straightforward and never wavered from his commitment to brand standards and absolute integrity.

As we gained more experience, we eventually had to find our own paths to leadership and decide what we wanted from our McDonald's careers. As fate would have it, in the late 1990s, we faced a significant setback in our journey as franchise owners; this was the turning point that changed our trajectory forever.

One of the biggest challenges of being a McDonald's franchisee is the lack of control over the territory in which you operate. The franchise agreement allows you to own and operate a McDonald's only at the specific address of your location. As a result, the McDonald's Corporation has the power to develop sites around your area and choose any ownership it desires. This freedom gives the corporation a tremendous amount of leverage over its franchisees. If you're not performing or not aligned with McDonald's Corporation's vision, the company can make you ineligible for growth or even not rewrite your franchise agreement beyond the typical twenty-year term. When the corporation builds a new restaurant, it can allow another franchisee to run it, regardless of the new restaurant's proximity to your location.

In the mid-1990s a McDonald's site was being developed near my father's market, which was an excellent opportunity for us to grow. However, due to the lack of territorial rights, we had to campaign intensely for a few years to be awarded the new location. Unfortunately, the McDonald's Corporation's final decision was to give it to a neighboring owner/operator. This news was disappointing for us, and we were left feeling angry, bitter, and disillusioned by the entire process.

The decision to award the location to someone else had a significant impact on all of us, but especially on our father. He had been an owner/operator for almost thirty years and thus felt a deep sense of bitterness and betrayal, which led him to consciously distance himself from the day-to-day business of McDonald's. This decision forced my brother and me to make a tough career choice: we could continue feeling sour and angry, or we could adopt a fresh perspective on how to succeed in our careers. We could follow our father's path or chart our own course.

> "To each, there comes in their lifetime a
> special moment when they are figuratively tapped on
> the shoulder and offered the chance to do a very special
> thing, unique to them and fitted to their talents.
> What a tragedy if that moment finds them
> unprepared or unqualified for that which
> could have been their finest hour."
> —WINSTON CHURCHILL[13]

We realized that the times and franchisee expectations had changed significantly from our father's early days, and in order to succeed, we needed to accept these changes and adapt to them. For example, one reason our father had not been awarded the new location was that he was not politically connected in the McDonald's community. He had chosen not to actively participate in the various owner/operator leadership associations that partnered with McDonald's to drive the business forward. In the end, he did not have the necessary relationships with the key decision-makers of the day. He lost the opportunity to create goodwill with the people who facilitated decisions.

After much discussion, we decided to become owner/operators who were different from our father. This meant that we had to

---

[13] Quoted in Ryan Holiday, *Courage Is Calling: Fortune Favors the Brave* (New York: Portfolio, 2021), 28.

make sacrifices, such as spending more time traveling and away from our own organization. But we believed it was the best choice for us; we needed to build something beyond our father's legacy. Our decision eventually led to great opportunities, such as owning more locations than we'd ever imagined and forging relationships with McDonald's corporate executives and other owners across the country.

At first, when the corporation awarded the new site to another owner/operator, we were disheartened by the missed opportunity, yet it turned out to be a defining moment in our careers. It made us realize our own career truth, and we have drawn on this experience as well as other temporary defeats over the past twenty-five years.

Every time you encounter setbacks, the way is paved for other opportunities that you may not have discovered otherwise.

CHAPTER 8

Goodness

"No beauty shines brighter than that of a good heart."
—SHANINA SHAIK

IN ADDITION TO CREATING AND SEEKING OUT BEAUTY AND FINDING and living our truth, to seek excellence, we must allow the truth to lead to something deeper and more meaningful: goodness, the third and final essential transcendental virtue.

The Principle of Beneficence

Those who study applied and professional ethics are familiar with the principle of beneficence, which encompasses all norms, dispositions, and actions that have the goal of benefiting or promoting the good of other persons. The principle describes an obligation to aim for optimal contribution to others and society—in short, to aim for goodness.

The principle of beneficence can be summed up in the Golden Rule, which instructs individuals to treat others in the same way that they would like to be treated. This means that we should practice ethical maximalism by behaving in ways that produce the largest number of good consequences. This is different from Aristotle's Silver Rule, which only requires individuals to refrain from harming others based on what they would not want done to themselves. The Golden Rule is proactive and commands us to "do unto others," instead of simply avoiding harm to others. It represents the magnanimity of a spirit that leads to the virtue of goodness.

> "Impartiality, the main ingredient of morality,
> is not just a logical nicety. Practically speaking, it also
> makes everyone, on average, better off. Life presents many
> opportunities to help someone, or to refrain from hurting
> them, at a small cost to oneself. So if everyone signs
> on to helping and not hurting, everyone wins.
> This does not, of course, mean that people are in fact
> perfectly moral, just that there's a rational
> argument as to why they should be."
> —STEVEN PINKER, cognitive psychologist at Harvard University

Pinker, a renowned Harvard psychologist and an avowed atheist, argues that goodness can be explained through rationality and reason rather than religion or God. According to him, moral virtue is the logical way to foster harmony within a community and how we communicate the truth in our daily lives and relationships.

Conveying goodness means recognizing others' work, partnering, and being selfless, generous, respectful, empathetic, just, and purposeful. It involves living a meaningful and fulfilling life for oneself and others.

This concept applies to all organizations, including McDonald's. To attract and retain talented employees, we create beauty: we remodel the workplace and keep it clean and organized to make it appealing. However, simply having a shiny new building is not enough. We must also implement our truth—maintaining brand standards through practical training—by providing programs that help our employees grow and develop. Finally, to truly achieve excellence, we must practice goodness toward our people so they feel valued and listened to, which creates loyal and hardworking employees. We must create a welcoming, respectful, inclusive, and hospitable culture by being empathetic, consistently rewarding and recognizing good work, and challenging others to be their best.

In other words, we can have the best systems and processes in place and provide state-of-the-art training to our employees, but if we don't treat them with kindness and respect, we're not providing them with the goodness they ultimately need to thrive.

Biblical Wisdom

The concept that we must practice goodness to be effective leaders is supported biblically as well. The following verses from the New Testament speak to the responsibility of leadership.

"Then said Jesus to the crowds and to his disciples,
The scribes and the Pharisees sit on Moses' seat; so practice
and observe whatever they tell you, but not what they do;
for they preach, but do not practice. They bind heavy
burdens, hard to bear, and lay them on men's shoulders;
but they themselves will not move them with their finger.

They do all their deeds to be seen by men; for they
make their phylacteries broad and their fringes long, and
they love the place of honor at feasts and the best seats
in the synagogues, and salutations in the market places,
and being called rabbi by men. But you are not to be called
rabbi, for you have one teacher, and you are all brethren.
And call no man your father on earth, for you have one Father,
who is in heaven. Neither be called masters, for you have one
master, the Christ. He who is greatest among you shall be
your servant; whoever exalts himself will be humbled,
and whoever humbles himself will be exalted."

—MATTHEW 23: 1–12 (Revised Standard Version)

While this passage is particularly directed at religious leaders, its underlying principles are applicable to leadership in any context, whether it be in politics, business, education, or other areas of life. Leaders are called to be servants, to prioritize the well-being of those they lead, and to avoid the trappings of pride and self-centeredness. By doing so, they can fulfill their roles more effectively and make a positive impact on the lives of others.

Ultimately, the message encourages all individuals in positions of authority to reflect on their motivations, values, and actions and to strive to lead with integrity and humility for the greater good of those they are responsible for.

Practicing Goodness

For leaders, practicing goodness is essential to creating an enjoyable, productive workplace. If your employees feel belittled, disrespected, and expendable, they will not perform at their highest levels—and your employee turnover rate will be high. Disgruntled employees lead to substandard customer service, which leads to a drop in sales. As with beauty and truth, individual goodness leads to organizational goodness. If you can express your truth through goodness, your employees will shine and customer satisfaction will rise.

An excellent example of a leader who practiced goodness through servant leadership is the missionary Mother Teresa. She was a remarkable woman whose life and work have left an indelible mark on the world. As a young Catholic nun, she journeyed to India, where she spent five decades working tirelessly in the poorest slum in the world. Despite the unconscionable conditions, Mother Teresa dedicated herself to caring for those on the brink of death, offering them comfort, compassion, and love in their darkest hours.

Her selflessness and charitable heart made her one of the most beautiful women in the world. Her unwavering commitment to serving others, even in the direst circumstances, earned her the admiration and respect of people from all walks of life. Mother Teresa's impact was so profound that she was eventually canonized as a saint by the Catholic Church.

It's incredible to think that acts of kindness, truth, and selflessness can have such a profound impact on the world. Late in her life, Mother Teresa became one of the most influential and well-known figures in the world, based on her radiant expression of beauty, truth, and goodness. As the saying goes, beauty attracts, truth convinces, but goodness affirms. Mother Teresa embodied this goodness in the most extraordinary way. She is a testament to the power of human kindness and compassion.

May we all be inspired by Mother Teresa's example and strive to live our lives with integrity, making our journey mutually rewarding for ourselves and those around us.

Expressing Goodness through Mentorship

As a leader, part of practicing goodness is mentoring your employees. This means actively providing them guidance on how to perform at a higher level. Recognizing a job well done is wonderful, but providing specific advice and constructive criticism in an encouraging tone of voice goes a long way too.

As the leader of a responsible organization, you have the duty to hold your employees accountable for their performance. This might involve having difficult conversations and documenting their progress, but such measures ultimately help them grow in a new direction and improve their overall work performance. Your goal should be to "coach up" your people to help them advance in the organization—or even to "coach out" your people so they leave your organization with better skills than they had when they began. This approach fosters equal opportunities for all employees rather than equal outcomes.

McDonald's director Daniel describes the coach-up or coach-out philosophy in the following excerpt from his interview. He mentions how his former manager mentored him and how he, in turn, mentors his people.

I had a guy that I worked with for three months, but you'd have thought I worked for him for three years based on the difference he made in my life. I made a difference in his, too, but we didn't know it at the time. You don't know what length of time you'll be working with people, but it doesn't matter—make it a good experience. Somebody's going to talk about it later.

The values and the skills that McDonald's teaches an employee—whether they're going to be with us a month, a year, the length of time doesn't matter because we give it to them on day one—those skills will carry them through. We have little business phrases like, "Clean as you go," and "You got time to lean, you got time to clean." If you make a mess, you clean it up. We want you to be at work on time, ready to go. We're going to hold you accountable to that if your attendance is not good. We're going to call you out on it. We're going to talk to you about it. You may not be working for us if you can't get here on time. Teaching core skillsets like that, little values, stick with people the rest of their lives. If a customer comes in, we want you to smile at the customer. They're paying our bills. They're the reason why we're here. For those folks that want to grow, we try to paint them a picture: if you do a great job, you will excel to higher levels. But you have to do a great job. It's about planting those seeds.

Make your people better than when they come in. Make them better as they go out. You want to make sure the environment is one in which people are nurtured and can grow and have something to take with them if they do go. We want to recognize the crew and reward them for a job well done. When crew members become bosses in whatever business they go into, hopefully, they're going to take care of their people, recognizing a job well done, the way we took care of them.

Daniel also describes how McDonald's, and the mentorship he received there, was his bridge from poverty to leadership.

I grew up very poor in the hills of Kentucky. We lived in a two-bedroom house with no heat, even in the winter, and no running water. We had wells and an outhouse. There was little food to go around. If it wasn't for the Catholic Church, we would have gone hungry. We had a big family. It was bad.

I was twelve years old when I tasted my first McDonald's hamburger. My family lived in Kent, and there wasn't a restaurant around us. We saw commercials on our old black and white TV, but I'd never seen one in person. One day I went to a competition with my choir a couple of hours away. We stopped at a McDonald's. "I can't believe I'm here!" I thought. "I've seen this on TV!" I had my first Big Mac with a caramel sundae. It was heavenly. You have to remember, I didn't have that kind of exposure as a kid. We never ate out. Restaurants were only things I saw on television, so that moment stuck with me.

Lord have mercy, would anyone know that a few years later I'd be working at McDonald's?

When I was fourteen, after my father cracked me with a baseball bat during an argument, I ran away from home to live in Norwood, Ohio, with my older half-sister, Geri. I got my first McDonald's job as a crew kid while living with her, when I was sixteen. I needed money to take the girl I was dating to prom, so when I went into our local McDonald's and saw a big sign on the wall that said, "Now Hiring Smiling Faces," I filled out an application, the GM interviewed me, and I was hired. I never dreamed I'd be here forty years later.

At first what drove me to work at McDonald's was that I could make money: $3.15/hour, which was a lot back then. I was able to go to prom with my girlfriend (a relationship that lasted for far less time than my job). I kept twenty dollars from every paycheck for myself and put the rest in the bank. I was able to pay for Geri to get a lawyer to get guardianship of me. Slowly, my other brothers and sisters started migrating to us, and I paid for them to get guardianship. Eventually, my mom and dad came to Norwood as well. By then my career path was well started.

But the money became a by-product of working there. I stayed because I loved it. It was a fun job, not work I dreaded. I liked everyone I worked with. I felt like I was part of something, a feeling I had never had before. It impacted me subconsciously in a way I only now realize as I reflect back today. They made me feel welcome when I joined the team and gave me a good foundation at my orientation. Then they continued helping me through hands-on training, coaching, and mentorship. The guy I first worked for owned forty restaurants, and he included me in conversations about his success and how to build it. He made me feel like I was part of something important.

Back then, I had no clue why I loved it, but I was the person willing to come into work whenever they needed help. If they needed me to open. If they needed me to close. If they needed me to work a double shift. My answer was always, "Whatever you need." The job was my world.

I stayed at McDonald's because I believe when you like what you do, keep doing it. I loved McDonald's from day one. Every day was different. The acknowledgment that I was doing a good job and performing well, that I was part of something greater, kept me going. It's a great gig.

McDonald's supervisor Jonathon expresses what mentorship means to him.

What sets McDonald's apart in culture is the type of people who work here. For many, it's their first job. McDonald's offers a support system that many people may not have had. I have to say I'm a perfect example of that. Nobody in my life told me they believed in me. I never had a coach, a teacher, or a parent say, "Do this," or push me to "do that" until my first boss, Elton. And I feel like that is what a lot of people, especially younger individuals, might be missing in their lives. That teacher. That coach. That person in your life that you look back on and you're like, "Wow, that person made a difference in my life." That's what I'm trying to be to a lot of my guys.

In addition to practicing goodness by personally mentoring your employees, you can provide more formal, structured mentorship at the organization level as well. Our LEAD program, started several years ago, is a wonderful example.

LEAD (Leadership, Education, Advancement, Development) was created internally to help identify and facilitate future McDonald's leaders as well as those interested in using McDonald's as a bridge to leadership elsewhere. The central theme of the program is "try to be better tomorrow than we are today." We encourage participants to make a conscious choice to think about their short- and long-term goals...and to not be afraid to dream. We constantly preach the idea of McDonald's as a bridge. To date, we have helped hundreds of people reach their leadership dreams.

CHAPTER 9

Embodying the Transcendental Virtues

"Success is not final, failure is not fatal:
it is the courage to continue that counts."

—WINSTON CHURCHILL

NOW THAT WE UNDERSTAND THE TRUE MEANING OF THE TRAN-
scendental virtues of beauty, truth, and goodness, let's talk about
how important it is to embody them. Every day, we need to remind
ourselves of what beauty truly means to us—not just the concept
of beauty as seen in social media, television, and movies, but the
unique beauty that sets us apart from the rest of society. We must
also focus daily on conveying our truth and providing goodness
to achieve excellence in all aspects of our lives.

Biblical Wisdom

In 2011, I had the opportunity to visit the Holy Land on a pil-
grimage with the Dynamic Catholic organization. This trip was

a life-changing event for me as I could finally connect biblical stories with specific geographies. Now when I read or hear these biblical stories, I can visualize and remember the locations and their proximity to each other, so they have a deeper impact on me. Even after a decade, I still like to tease my children by saying "I've been there" after Mass. It's a way of reminiscing and reminding myself of how fortunate I am to have walked on the same soil that Christ and his apostles did.

One location we visited was the Mount of Beatitudes in Israel, traditionally thought to be where Jesus delivered his famous Sermon on the Mount (though the exact location is a matter of historical interpretation). This hillside is near the Sea of Galilee, close to the town of Capernaum. At the top of the hill sits the Church of the Beatitudes, built in the 1930s. Each wall of this octagonal Roman Catholic church represents one of the eight Beatitudes—sayings of Jesus, as recounted by his apostles in Scripture. As I sat in this serene spot and contemplated God's message and wisdom, I understood that the Beatitudes reflect the importance of embodying the transcendental virtues.

The Beatitudes—KJV
Matthew 5:3–12

Blessed are the poor in spirit: for theirs is the kingdom of heaven.

Blessed are they that mourn: for they shall be comforted.

Blessed are the meek: for they shall inherit the earth.

Blessed are they which do hunger & thirst after righteousness: for they shall be filled.

Blessed are the merciful: for they shall obtain mercy.

Blessed are the pure in heart: for they shall see God.

Blessed are the peacemakers: for they shall be called the children of God.

Blessed are they which are persecuted for righteousness' sake: for theirs is the kingdom of heaven.

The Beatitudes are a foundational component of Christianity and moral ethics, serving as a cornerstone that reinforces the power of beauty, truth, and goodness. Christ proclaimed them at the beginning of his ministry, emphasizing their crucial role in building his Church. However, in our current times, we tend to overlook the essence of these ideas, often dismissing them as either anti-capitalist propaganda or incompatible with our philosophy of strong leadership. We have discarded words like *meek* and *righteous*, considering them unappealing and outdated. However, we forget that meekness is unrelated to submission and righteousness is not synonymous with pomposity or smugness. The meek, in fact, perceive beauty through the lens of God, while the righteous abide by *the* truth rather than their truth. The peacemakers are not compromisers; they are individuals who consistently seek to manifest goodness through their actions. Living the transcendental virtues requires a buy-in to the humility and selflessness that the Beatitudes convey.

Throughout my career, I have had the privilege of working with many dynamic and talented individuals who had the potential to bring about significant positive change within the restaurant organization. However, there were a few among them who chose to prioritize their own interests and personal gain over those of the company or the McDonald's brand. This misalignment of motivation ultimately led to their downfall, as they ended up compromising the best interests of the company for their own benefit. I have witnessed such individuals steal money and justify it by convincing themselves they were underpaid. I've seen them manipulate data to present themselves in a better light or to cover up mistakes. This kind of unethical and illegal behavior boils down to misaligned priorities and a lack of commitment to organizational truth.

"Finally, brothers and sisters, whatever is true,
whatever is noble, whatever is right, whatever is pure,
whatever is lovely, whatever is admirable—if anything is
excellent or praiseworthy—think about such things."
—PHILIPPIANS 4:8 (New International Version)

Sacrifice

In order to embody the transcendental virtues, we must not only be willing to sacrifice, but we must also view sacrifice as a necessary part of the journey.

"God writes straight with crooked lines."
—Often attributed to ST. TERESA OF ÁVILA

This saying means that though our lives often seem to be filled with difficulty and tragedy, God can use it all to achieve His greater purpose. In today's world, where noise and distractions have become the norm, we may have lost sight of the greater purpose of this life and this journey. The reality is that we will all suffer and must be willing to make a proper sacrifice today for a greater good tomorrow.

Over the past seven years, I have been intrigued by the work of Jordan Peterson, a renowned clinical psychologist and professor who has made a significant mark on our culture via his books and YouTube videos. Though I knew the Old Testament biblical stories well from a theological perspective, through Peterson's podcasts and YouTube lectures I have grasped the deep psychological brilliance of these stories. His lectures on the narratives of Job and Cain and

Abel are examples of beautiful metaphors that transcend time and space but stand as meta-stories for how we live and see the world regardless of the generation in which we live.

The story of Job is about a man who loses everything—his wealth, health, family, respect—yet ultimately keeps his faith in God. Eventually, God restores what he had twofold. This story tackles a basic human question: Why should I dedicate my life to goodness when there seems to be no reward or benefit? I must admit that this is a struggle for me. Over the course of my career, I have faced numerous challenges, including internal and external theft, false and frivolous lawsuits, and countless other injustices that have caused me monumental anguish, stress, and expense. Many of us struggle with similar feelings, which create a barrier in our journey for excellence. The story of Job's determination to maintain his faith and integrity, even in the face of trials, tribulations, and extreme suffering, serves as a powerful reminder of the importance of perseverance and moral strength in the face of adversity.

In the ancient biblical story of Cain and Abel, we learn about two brothers who each presented God a sacrifice as an expression of devotion. God shows favor to Abel because his sacrifice (the best of his flock) was more sincere and of higher quality than his brother's sacrifice. Cain feels rejected and jealous, which leads to anger. Eventually, he kills Abel in a fit of jealousy and is punished by God for his crime. This story carries several themes, including lack of personal accountability for the consequences of second-tier sacrifice. Cain was not willing to accept that Abel's greater sacrifice justified the reward he received from God. He was caught up in comparison culture, and his jealousy turned to hatred and violence, leading him to live a life of envy and bitterness.

"Embrace the suck."

—US MARINES

This quip was popularized in 2003 by US Marines in Iraq. In a crude way, it embodies one of the ideas propagated in Jordan Peterson's work. Peterson believes leading a life that is both fulfilling and purposeful requires us to be willing to make proper sacrifices. These sacrifices may involve forgoing immediate gratification, comfort, or even one's own ego, all for the sake of achieving a greater good or a brighter future. Peterson's main objective is to inspire young people to take control of their lives, confront challenges head-on, and make the necessary sacrifices to achieve meaningful and rewarding goals. According to Peterson, sacrifice is not just about giving up something; it is an essential element in personal growth and the discovery of meaning in life.

Peterson's study of sacrifice is closely linked with his thoughts about the significance of purpose, accountability, and what he calls the "hero's journey." He believes we are all capable and called to be heroes as we journey through this life. As Milton Friedman said, "There's no such thing as a free lunch." We must be willing to embrace the suck—to accept suffering as a redemptive experience and make the proper sacrifices for others and ourselves—if we are ever to embody beauty, truth, and goodness.

Disneyland versus Disney Corporation

In this book, I have consistently used McDonald's as an example to illustrate the complexities of business operations and strategies that align with my premise. However, to make a stronger case for how implementing the principles of beauty, truth, and goodness can drive excellence in the business world, let's delve into another renowned brand from the golden age of the 1950s.

Disneyland, located in Anaheim, California, is a world-renowned theme park that has captured the hearts and imaginations of millions of people worldwide. It is a shining example of how the integration of beauty, truth, and goodness can shape a successful enterprise and enhance and bond a culture of people.

Walt Disney conceived the idea of Disneyland while sitting on a park bench in Griffith Park, Los Angeles, watching his daughters play. He envisioned a place where children and adults could have fun together, a park that would be clean, safe, and entertaining for all ages. His inspirational vision of this beauty stimulated his brilliant idea.[14]

The construction of Disneyland began in 1954, led by Walt Disney and a team of designers, architects, and artists. Transforming orange groves into his magical kingdom was a massive undertaking. The attention to detail was remarkable, with every aspect of the park carefully crafted to create an immersive experience for visitors. Disneyland opened its doors to the public on July 17, 1955, and, as Paul Harvey would say, "now you know the rest of the story!"

Over the years, Disneyland expanded and introduced new attractions, including Adventureland, Frontierland, Fantasyland, and Tomorrowland. Eventually, New Orleans Square, Critter Country, and Mickey's Toontown were added. Walt Disney was actively involved in the park's design and development, aiming to create a place that constantly evolved and improved.

---

[14] Jim Denney, "The Origin of Walt's Disneyland Idea," Walt's Disneyland, May 3, 2017, https://waltsdisneyland.wordpress.com/2017/05/03/the-origin-of-walts-disneyland-idea/.

Disneyland changed the theme park industry by setting a new standard for integrating beauty, truth, and goodness into its business model. Disney's genius was creating a consistently amazing and beautiful experience that attracts people of all ages, generation after generation. The emphasis on storytelling provides a unique opportunity to convey the best of American culture and values. The amazing hospitality and attention to detail create a sense of goodness that completes the experience.

In stark contrast to Disneyland is its current parent company, the Walt Disney Corporation. The company is utterly lost in defining its mission and purpose. The foundation of Disneyland was nostalgic American culture based on family values, but the Walt Disney Corporation has radically abandoned that strategy across most of its media platforms. It is, however, unable to align on what the foundational replacement should be. The company seems to be rudderless in its pursuit of this replacement, often switching direction with the temporal cultural winds of the moment. It has no clear direction of what constitutes beauty; there is absolutely no foundation of consistent truth and, thus, no dependable societal goodness. In fact, millions of people claim the exact opposite.

The Tapestry of Our Lives

Corrie ten Boom, a Dutch woman known for her courageous actions during World War II, is another example of someone who embodied the transcendental virtues of beauty, truth, and goodness.[15] Her story is one of faith, resilience, and heroism.

---

[15] Karisa You, "Life as a Tapestry: The Miracle-Filled Life of Corrie ten Boom," SOLA Network, September 13, 2022, https://sola.network/article/the-miracle-filled-life-of -corrie-ten-boom/.

Born on April 15, 1892, in Haarlem, Netherlands, Corrie came from a devout Christian family that ran a watchmaker's shop in their home. Corrie and her family were known for their deep faith and commitment to helping others. During the Nazi occupation of the Netherlands in World War II, the ten Boom family began providing a safe haven for Jews and members of the Dutch resistance in their home. They constructed a secret hiding place behind a false wall in Corrie's bedroom. This secret room, barely large enough for a few people to stand, became a sanctuary for those fleeing persecution.

In February 1944, the ten Boom family was betrayed to the Nazis, and their home was raided. Corrie; her father, Casper; and her sister, Betsie, were arrested and sent to various concentration camps. Corrie and Betsie ended up at the notorious Ravensbrück concentration camp in Germany. Despite the deplorable conditions and constant threat of death, Corrie and Betsie remained steadfast in their faith and their commitment to helping others. Betsie's kindness and Corrie's determination to share hope and love with their fellow prisoners made a profound impact.

Tragically, Betsie passed away in Ravensbrück, but Corrie miraculously survived. After her release, she dedicated her life to sharing her story and promoting forgiveness and reconciliation. She traveled the world, speaking about her experiences and the power of forgiveness, even forgiving one of the former Ravensbrück guards who had mistreated her.

Corrie ten Boom's autobiography, *The Hiding Place*, was published in 1971 and was later turned into a movie. Corrie became a well-known Christian speaker and author, and her life's work was a testament to the strength of the human spirit and the capacity for forgiveness in the face of unimaginable suffering.

Corrie ten Boom passed away on her ninety-first birthday—April 15, 1983—leaving a legacy of compassion, faith, and resilience that continues to inspire people around the world. Corrie included a beautiful and poignant poem in her book that aligns with her message of trusting in God's plan, even when we cannot see the full picture.

THE WEAVING

My life is but a weaving
Between my God and me.
I cannot choose the colors
He weaveth steadily.
Oft' times He weaveth sorrow;
And I in foolish pride
Forget He sees the upper
And I the underside.
Not 'til the loom is silent
And the shuttles cease to fly
Will God unroll the canvas
And reveal the reason why.
The dark threads are as needful
In the weaver's skillful hand
As the threads of gold and silver
In the pattern He has planned
He knows, He loves, He cares;
Nothing this truth can dim.
He gives the very best to those
Who leave the choice to Him.

—GRANT COLFAX TULLAR (1869–1950)

This poem encapsulates the idea that every thread in the tapestry of life, whether light or dark, is essential in God's grand design. The poem's message serves as a source of inspiration for those facing trials and difficulties, much like Corrie's own experiences during her time in the concentration camps.

It is only through humility and faith that we can hope to weather all the storms we'll experience over the course of our lifetime. There will always be strife, mental and physical sickness, despair, betrayal, concupiscence, and loneliness. Being able to see beyond the individual sorrows and transgressions of life takes a tremendous amount of fortitude, courage, virtue, and faith in something far greater than our ability to understand, yet that is what we are called to do. How often do we look back at our own lives, twenty or thirty years earlier, and feel thankful we didn't get what we desired back then? How often can we look back on a tragedy many years later and begin to see some greater purpose or personal growth?

In her book, Corrie often uses two images to reinforce her message. The first depicts the back of a tapestry, which appears to be a chaotic mess of threads arranged in a disorderly fashion. This represents the seeming randomness of life. In contrast, the second image shows the front view of the tapestry, a beautiful visual representation of the message conveyed in the poem "The Weaving."

In my previous book, I delved into the challenging journey my wife, Kaaren, and I undertook, marked by years of infertility and marital struggles. During those years, I grappled with anger and bitterness, struggling to come to terms with the misfortune that seemed to plague us. The turmoil I felt is a part of the human condition—at least it was for me at the time. However, more than two decades later, all the hardships we endured have gradually melted away, revealing God's deeper purpose in my life's journey.

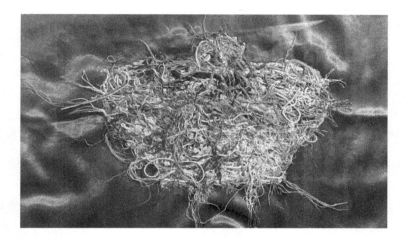

I couldn't envision a life without our children, true miracles in my life brought to fruition only through a series of unplanned and painful circumstances that affected many people. If we were to scrutinize each micro event in isolation, as we often do in the moment, we would perceive only struggle, anxiety, sorrow, and disappointment. But when viewed collectively, these seemingly disparate experiences come together to form the most beautiful tapestry imaginable.

I find myself in awe of the power of God when I contemplate life through this prism. Have you ever considered the seemingly isolated or individual events in your life that, in hindsight, you see were woven together with others to create the magic you now have in your life? By meditating on these incredible mysteries, we can step outside ourselves in moments of pride and negativity. This is a key element in embodying beauty, truth, and goodness, even through life's struggles.

The story of St. Maximilian Kolbe is another remarkable example of the intricate tapestry of our lives. He was a Polish Conventual Franciscan friar who was arrested and sent to German death camp at Auschwitz for aiding Jewish refugees during World War II. When ten men at the camp were randomly selected for execution as punishment for a prisoner escape, Kolbe volunteered to die in place of one of the men, who had a wife and young children. The Nazis withheld food from the ten men for weeks and then, on August 14, 1941, injected Kolbe and the others who had not yet died from starvation with carbolic acid.[16]

Kolbe's extraordinary selfless act of volunteering to die in place of a stranger is a testament to his indomitable courage and faith. Though he lived in complete obscurity during his lifetime, he is

---

[16] "Saint Maximilian Mary Kolbe," Franciscan Media, 10/15/23, accessed May 29, 2024, https://www.franciscanmedia.org/saint-of-the-day/saint-maximilian-mary-kolbe/.

now infinitely famous, and his impact on the world is undeniable. His ostensibly inconspicuous act of heroism has transcended time and borders; he has become a globally renowned symbol of sacrifice. His actions have inspired millions of people to recognize the power of courage and faith over the darkest forces of sin and death. He met his end in 1941, but his legacy endured. Pope John Paul II recognized Kolbe's sanctity and canonized him as a saint and martyr of charity on October 10, 1982. Every August 14, the world commemorates his life, and his valor continues to rekindle our spirits.

In the face of negativity, despair, and cowardice, we can see the stories of Corrie ten Boom and St. Maximilian Kolbe as guiding lights. They exemplify how faith and unwavering dedication to living the transcendental virtues can overcome adversity, whether within our own families, in the workplace, or in any other endeavors.

Dying with Beauty, Truth, and Goodness

Not only does embodying the transcendental virtues allow you to achieve excellence in life, but doing so can allow you to achieve excellence in death as well. I experienced this personally when my father passed away.

As of late 2023, the Centers for Disease Control and Prevention reports that 108,298,645 people in the United States contracted COVID-19 and 1,181,289 lost their lives to the virus—in other words, roughly 1 percent of those who got COVID-19 died. The vast majority of those who died were already medically compromised or well beyond seventy years of age. My father fell into this category. In 2021, he was eighty-five and grappling with early-onset diabetes, hypertension, and heart disease, making him highly susceptible, even after receiving vaccines.

My father's hospitalization is a poignant example of one of the great tragedies of our time. Family members were most often barred from visiting their loved ones at hospitals during the pandemic, and thus were unable to provide essential care and emotional support. This isolation took a toll on patients, as being surrounded by the people they love could have been a crucial source of strength and motivation.

In my father's case, we were not allowed to visit him until the very last day of his hospital stay, when the doctors assumed his passing was imminent. My mother sat by his bedside as all his children and grandchildren hurried to the hospital to see him one last time and say their goodbyes. We were allowed into the hospital one at a time, and we each had to wear a cumbersome plastic suit to enter his room. With all the visitors, it turned into a bit of a zoo! However, the hospital staff was very accommodating of our final request. As we took turns going in, we staged a vigil outside the hospital, praying, comforting, and telling stories of my father's impact on our lives.

After all the visits, expressions of love, and heartfelt goodbyes, my father showed remarkable resilience, enough for the family to bring him home to hospice care. During the last three days of his life, he was surrounded by my mother, his children, and his grandchildren. We sang, prayed, and showered him with love until he peacefully passed on to the next life a day before his eighty-sixth birthday. The experience, though undoubtedly brutal, also contained moments of profound beauty, truth, and goodness.

Organizational Embodiment of Transcendental Virtues

Just as an individual can embody beauty, truth, and goodness, so can an organization as a whole. As a leader, when you embrace these transcendental virtues, you create a mission-driven organization that achieves excellence.

McDonald's supervisor Jonathon describes how he creates a mission-driven organization.

Life is short, so I try to make the job as enjoyable as possible for everyone. Here it can sometimes feel like a revolving door. We're often a bridge for a lot of people, like John always says—a bridge to somewhere else. And that's fine. But it means a lot of employees come through. They're nervous. They're young. I remember my first day. I was nervous and I didn't want to come back. So I try to put my employees at ease as much as I can.

We have to make the job fun and enjoyable for the people coming in and make them feel valued. They're people, and everybody has things that affect them differently. I try to treat everybody with respect, to listen to them as best I can and tap into what drives them. I figure out how I can motivate them personally, whether it's Maria, who's been doing the lobby at Olive Avenue for thirty years, or our owner/operator. I just try to tap into how they think and how I can help them get better.

In this business, every day is different. Today can go so smoothly, and tomorrow could be hell. Everything could blow up. Stores could lose power. People could quit. To get through the challenges you have to be at your best for everybody around you every day. The other night, I was visiting one of my stores when a car died in the drive-thru, which meant we weren't going to make our service time goal. But we didn't give up. We discussed it. "How can we adapt and overcome?" So we went outside and pushed the car out of the drive-thru. Boom! It was done. It's so easy to throw up the white flag and give up when bad things happen, but you have to keep a positive attitude and figure it out.

I try to push people to adapt and overcome because everybody has challenges. Everybody has issues. Everybody has a past. But in this business, it's how you deal with those things that will make you or break you.

CHAPTER 10

Executing a Life of Vocation

"Every man has a vocation to be someone:
but he must understand clearly that in order to fulfill
this vocation he can only be one person: himself."

—THOMAS MERTON

MANY TIMES, WHEN I SPEAK TO GROUPS ABOUT STRIVING FOR EXCEL-
lence by embracing beauty, truth, and goodness, people wonder
if my ideas apply to them. They understand what I teach in the
context of my job as an owner/operator, with many people working
for me, but they aren't sure if it applies to their jobs, which are
typically of a much different capacity and scale.

Do you see your work as a job—something you have to do to
make money—or as a vocation—something you are called to do
to make a difference in the world? Certain professions, where the
work itself has a direct and substantial impact, serving the greater
good—such as doctor, nurse, schoolteacher, first responder, pastor

or priest, and public servant—inherently carry a profound sense of purpose or intrinsic meaning. But any profession, even those that do not directly involve saving lives, addressing critical injustices, or combating world hunger, can be a vocation. Our task is to imbue our work with intrinsic value and deep meaning, whatever the work may be.

For example, though many in society do not associate being a McDonald's owner/operator with vocation (in fact, I've had to contend with negative press, primarily due to the pseudoscientific documentary *Super Size Me* and the mockumentary *Fast Food Nation*), I find genuine purpose and satisfaction in my role of serving customers and representing the McDonald's brand. I've chosen to infuse my work with significance and contribute positively to the world through my actions. It's this choice that makes my work fulfilling and purposeful and gives it a deeper meaning.

As leaders, we are called to instill the concept of work as a deeper vocation in our people as well. We must show them that work is a platform where we can bring our unique talents and intrinsic value to the job. We should encourage them to discover their purpose and self-worth by both nurturing them and holding them accountable. We must provide flexibility and understanding to highlight the importance of prioritizing family. We should strive to motivate individuals by harnessing the power of reciprocity, and we should encourage them to do the same in their personal and professional lives. In doing so, we demonstrate that we all have the ability to imbue our work with meaning and make a positive impact on the world.

Why Vocation?

The etymology of *vocation* is from the Latin *vocatio*, literally "a calling, a being called." It is my firm belief that businesses and those who lead others are called to be a force for good. Recent studies show that the vast majority of business executives agree that in order to be successful, a company must have a purpose beyond mere profit. Now more than ever, people expect their companies to make a positive impact on individual lives, their organizations, and the world at large. A flourishing business cannot exist without flourishing people.[17] And to have flourishing people, you must teach them to view their jobs as vocations that warrant excellence and contain meaning.

Day by Day

Changing your mindset to view and treat your job as a deeper vocation requires embracing beauty, truth, and goodness—and that takes time. It does not happen magically but, rather, by a daily commitment to the process.

I vividly recall attending a Catholic young adult retreat with my family in 1972. My parents actively participated in the event, delivering talks aimed at young men and women about marriage, family, and relationships. It was a time when many teenagers were caught in the cultural whirlwind of the late 1960s and early 1970s, and sadly, many would face substantial challenges during that decade.

---

[17] Cheryl Fields Tyler, "Business as a Force for Good (Part One): What Does This Mean and Why Is It So Important Today?" *Forbes*, March 8, 2022, https://www.forbes.com /sites/forbesbusinesscouncil/2022/03/08/business-as-a-force-for-good-part-one-what -does-this-mean-and-why-is-it-so-important-today/?sh=640be9c26dd3.

Looking back more than fifty years later, I cherish the wonderful memories of that mountain retreat experience. That year was the peak of the Jesus movement that swept across America. The movie *Godspell* was released, and its theme song, "Day by Day," was particularly popular and thus was sung repeatedly during our retreat. Even now, that song can still evoke a swell of emotion in me. The song's power lies in the simplicity of its message:

> "Day by day, day by day, O dear Lord three things I pray;
> to see thee more clearly, to love thee more dearly,
> to follow thee more nearly, day by day."
> —"Day by Day," STEPHEN SCHWARTZ

Looking back on those words spoken long ago, I'm still convinced that they hold true to what many of us desire deep down in our hearts. The simplicity of the words *see Him more clearly, love Him more dearly, and follow Him more nearly* encapsulates the essence of a life well-lived in faith. It's a desire that I still hold dear: to have a clearer vision of God's presence in my life, to love Him more passionately, and to follow Him more intimately. But regardless of your personal spiritual views, these words are a reminder to focus on the present. Do your best each day without worrying about the next. If you fail at expressing goodness one day, try again the next.

I Love My McJob!

The term *McJob* originally referred to a job working at McDonald's but now, unfortunately, is slang for a low-paying, low-prestige job, usually at a fast-food restaurant, that requires little skill and offers little opportunity for advancement. This is an inaccurate and unfair way to view the opportunities that businesses like McDonald's can offer. In fact, these kinds of jobs can be a powerful bridge for your career and life, providing mentorship and support that help you achieve your goals.

We all want the same things—to find our purpose and self-worth. No matter how "lowly" or "lofty" our jobs are, we grow and build our self-worth by learning responsibility, feeling pride in our work, and gaining a sense of independence and purpose. We can find vocation in any job, including a fast-food job.

When we were kids, my brothers and I worked for our father at McDonald's for about three hours each Saturday, and he paid us minimum wage. Our job was cleaning up cigarette butts and baseboards. To this day, dirty baseboards are my brother Jim's pet peeve! I was cleaning the cigarette butts from a patio planter one day in 1976 when a lady approached me and said, "You're so cute! How much do they pay you?" I still remember being almost too embarrassed to tell her I was being paid the grand sum of $2.30 per hour. We were used to receiving a twenty-five-cent-per-week allowance from our mother for doing household chores, so $2.30 per hour seemed insanely extravagant.

Eventually, I was old enough to wear the uniform and work in the restaurant. Two to three days a week, from 3:30 to 7:00 p.m., I worked "lot and lobby," which meant sweeping and mopping the lobby, cleaning tables, and checking the parking lot. As a lowly rookie, I had to wear a bright yellow hat instead of one of the blue hats worn by most other employees or one of the red hats cocked just right on the confident heads of a select few. My yellow hat signaled to customers that I was still in training. After putting in time and passing a written test, I was promoted to crew person in good standing and allowed to wear a blue hat and work the fry station. I was so proud. Over the course of time, I learned all the stations of the restaurant well and was given the privilege of wearing the coveted red hat, the visible sign that I had been promoted to shift leader.

We had a lot of fun as teenagers working in the restaurants; we were not always the perfect employees. Before the days of workplace safety regulations, we used to challenge each other to see who could carry the most cases of meat up the basement stairs at one time. The cases weighed thirty pounds apiece, and we tried to carry three or four cases at a time! We also had contests to see who could punch the deepest hole in the shortening before placing it in the vat. Despite these shenanigans, most of us took pride in being the best grill person or order taker we could possibly be. Working there was a chance to learn responsibility, feel pride in our work, and make a few bucks. It gave us a sense of independence and purpose and helped build on our self-worth.

Inspiring employees to feel this way is harder now than when I was a teen for a few reasons: society as a whole disparages the "starter job" idea, the pandemic has lowered our standards and expectations for workers, and unearned governmental subsidies have mitigated the incentive to actually show up to work. Still, I believe that most employees today feel pride and accomplishment when they are treated well and their managers leverage beauty, truth, and goodness in their leadership styles.

These excerpts from interviews with McDonald's leaders address the misconceptions many people have about entry-level jobs in general and about working for a fast-food restaurant like McDonald's specifically. They show that working at any job can be a vocation.

Daniel—Forty Years at McDonald's

Most people believe McDonald's is a dead-end job for individuals lacking skills and [having] no other options. This belief frustrates me because McDonald's has provided everything in my life. I have been blessed with five amazing kids, eleven grandbabies, and a beautiful wife who has been with me through thick and thin. My current home is far from the two-bedroom house I grew up in with seven siblings, parents, dirt floors, holes in the wall, two wells for water, no vehicle, and no income. It's unbelievable to go from that to where I am today, all thanks to McDonald's.

The biggest misconception is that there's no career path at McDonald's. It's not true. I always try to change people's perspective on this as much as I can. McDonald's has made millionaires out of some, like the owner/operators today. They're multimillionaires, and people fail to comprehend that. Even as an employee, not an owner, an individual who works at McDonald's can be in the top 10 percent of income earners in the United States!

Even people who don't make careers at McDonald's have used it as a means to something better. It's impressive how many people have worked at McDonald's at some point in their lives. It used to be one in seven, but soon it might be one in nine or ten. When I meet people who used to work at McDonald's, I wonder what they learned and what they capitalized on to get where they are today.

When someone asks what I do for a living, I proudly show them my twenty-five-year service ring. I started as a crew member and worked my way up to become a director of operations after forty years of service.

Jerry—Thirty-Nine Years at McDonald's

When people learn what I do, they are often surprised. You can hear how sorry they are for me. But my job is a point of pride for me. When you live in a good neighborhood with a good car, and people ask what you do for a living, they expect something more glamorous. I lived in a neighborhood with a bunch of teachers and bank presidents. We'd have block parties outside, and everyone would talk about how hard it was to make ends meet. For me, it wasn't that hard. "So what do you do?" they'd ask. "I work at McDonald's." They couldn't believe it.

Our society needs more opportunities for young people to learn the importance of communication, hospitality, respect, responsibility, and sacrifice. Jobs like McDonald's offer these valuable life skills. At its best, the brand teaches the importance of attraction and the beauty of cooperation, kindness, cleanliness, organization, and service. At its best, the brand teaches the truth of beneficial training systems, integrity, sound policies, and consistent procedures. Lastly, at its best, the brand teaches the goodness of "golden" hospitality moments, selfless acts of kindness, empowering people to be better, and the power and grace in teamwork.

Elton—Thirty-Two Years at McDonald's

What people get wrong is thinking that McDonald's won't get you anywhere, that all you're going to do is flip burgers. But one in eight people have worked for McDonald's at some point in their lives. If anybody can flip burgers, I'd love to see those people come in and try it. It sounds easy enough, but first, we don't flip burgers anymore, and second, there's a process. I think people would be shocked to see all that really goes on behind the scenes to "flip a burger," from washing hands to sanitation to glove preparation—people have no idea. McDonald's isn't for everybody, and not everybody can do it. I've seen people tell me they can do it. I've given them an opportunity to, and some don't last long. The record is a lady who worked for me for two hours before she came to me and said, "I can't do this." People think it's easy when it's not. You've got to be an extremely talented person to multitask beyond belief. The people working the drive-thru are doing things you wouldn't believe, all at once and all by memory. I have watched my daughter take very large drive-thru orders while she's nowhere near the register. She'd memorize everything while she's doing who-knows-what and then go back and punch it in.

More importantly, I think what people get wrong about working for McDonald's is thinking that you're only going to be in an entry-level position. If you're willing to continue your development and put the work in, you'll go beyond entry level and see success. I've had two homes. I've been to Hawaii seven times in a row. People would be surprised at the things I've been able to do with my family from just "flipping burgers." Even if you don't want to advance, you can use the entry-level position to get you somewhere. For example, you might be working while you're still going to high school or working there part-time while you do something else. The job can bridge the gap to get you to your next goal.

Many of our hardworking employees have faced challenges in their lives, such as a lack of educational opportunities, lack of parental direction, or dealing with the consequences of poor choices as teenagers or young adults. For some, McDonald's may seem like a last resort, but that doesn't mean their work is any less important or valuable. Unfortunately, there is a pervasive cultural myth that entry-level jobs like those at McDonald's are dead-end positions with no chance for success. Much of this is due to a warped view of the definition of what constitutes success. This belief is both false and harmful, as it can make workers feel like their work is insignificant and that they are not worthy of pursuing their dreams. I believe it's my duty to help our team members see their work as meaningful and worthwhile. By doing so, we can help them build a bridge to a brighter future, where they can pursue their passions and achieve their goals.

Nurturing and Accountability

"I was an overnight success all right, but
thirty years is a long, long night."

—RAY KROC

Nobody achieves excellence immediately or in a vacuum. Young people, especially those starting their first jobs, need nurturing and accountability to begin treating their jobs as vocations. Understandably, they will make mistakes, but mature and wise leaders must nurture their young employees and hold them to the standards of truth and goodness.

"Failure is not the opposite of success, but part of it."

—ANONYMOUS

Over the past five years, I have had to come back time and again to the above words. I, like my employees, continue to make mistakes and struggle in "living out" the message in my day-to-day life—but I guess that's the whole point of the journey. It is worth ruminating on these words I wrote in my last book:

"The reality is that failure is inevitable and it's something we must all face. Continuing to move in a positive direction does not mean we will not face significant setbacks along the way. To overcome these setbacks and continue to move forward along our path toward holiness, we must be willing to embrace self-compassion as well. We are our own worst critics and worst enemies. We are all far too hard on ourselves. The self-loathing that follows our mistakes is extremely detrimental to our self-confidence, hope, and ultimate path to joy and happiness. We must embrace self-compassion."

—JOHN ABBATE, *Invest Yourself*

Biblical narratives contain divine wisdom that can provide us with insight and perspective on this subject. The story of St. Paul and the role of Barnabas illustrate the importance of encouragement and mentorship in our pursuit of excellence.

"Following Saul's [St. Paul's] conversion on the road to Damascus, he arrived in Jerusalem with hopes of joining the disciples. However, upon his arrival, the disciples were initially hesitant and fearful of Saul, as he had a reputation of being a persecutor of Christians. Despite this, Barnabas, who was known as the 'son of encouragement,' stepped forward and took Saul under his wing. He spoke to the apostles on Saul's behalf and recounted how Saul had encountered the Lord on the road and had been preaching fearlessly in Jesus' name in Damascus."

—ACTS 9:26–30

Barnabas believed wholeheartedly in the authenticity of Saul's conversion. His unwavering support and trust in Saul were crucial in integrating Saul into the Christian community, especially as others were skeptical and fearful of his past actions. Together, Barnabas and Saul traveled to Antioch, where they spent a considerable amount of time teaching and working with the growing community of believers. This story highlights the transformative power of reassurance and support in the lives of others, especially those who have experienced hardship in their lives.

Encouragement is vital in our business! That is why McDonald's started its LEAD program, which focuses on leadership, education, advancement, and development. Over the years, we have witnessed numerous employees grow and develop into general managers and supervisors and even explore other career paths that align better with their long-term aspirations. The program is designed to offer our employees a supportive environment and make the most of their time at McDonald's in a way that benefits both parties.

The following testimonial from McDonald's director Suki is a powerful example of how nurturing managers helped her turn her job into a vocation.

I came to the United States from India in 1990. I was twenty-one years old and did not know any English. Within six months, I got my first job, at McDonald's. I started with literally twenty dollars in my hand. I was trying to make a career, but it was tough to figure out the English. No one else at McDonald's was Indian or knew my language, Punjabi. I used to write down in Punjabi whatever my trainers and managers said to me, and I'd come home and ask either my husband or sister-in-law what it meant so I was prepared for my job the next day.

I was just a normal employee for the first five years, doing all the jobs I had learned to do. That's all I thought I could do, so I kept doing it. But my managers saw potential in me. They asked me if I would like to become a shift manager. I laughed at them. "I don't know English!" I said.

"I didn't ask you if you knew English or not," my boss said. "We believe you can lead a ten-person team."

"Okay," I said. "If that's what you think, then okay, I'll be a manager." And they gave me that position. That built my confidence and I thought, Wow, if I can do this, I can learn more.

I started growing at McDonald's. I worked all the levels, from shift manager to first assistant. Then one day, my managers asked me if I wanted to take over the restaurant as store manager. Again, I was like, "What are you saying? That's a lot of work. That's a lot of admin stuff. You have to go to meetings and this and that. I don't know if I can do that with my English."

Again, they said, "We didn't ask you if you knew English. We know you can run a restaurant."

"I need time to think," I said.

But they didn't give me time. They insisted I could do it. They gave me the key. "Go for it," they said. So I managed a store for five years. My managers saw my work ethic and wanted me to go to different restaurants that needed to be fixed. I wanted to stay at my restaurant, but they said, "No, we need help here. We know you can do it." After five years of store managing, they wanted me to interview for the supervisor position. I didn't hesitate for that one.

In the five years I was a supervisor, I ran five or six restaurants and five or six GMs reported to me throughout. Three of those years I was nominated for number one supervisor in the US. That was a kick for me. Wow, I did it!

Then came an opportunity to work in the corporate office. So I interviewed for that and got that position. Everywhere I worked, I focused on delivering and providing my people resources to be successful. When corporate had a reorganization, I began looking to work for an owner/operator. I had five interviews with five different owners in one day. I decided to work for John because, in the interview, he said, "Tell me a little about yourself." Then he said, "We don't have a position for you, but we want you to come work for us. We'll figure it out."

At that point, I did not even think about money. What was important was that somebody was giving me the opportunity to show what I had. I'm so glad I made that decision. Now I am a director of operations, and he is helping me become an owner/operator. It's my American dream to own a business, so why not McDonald's with all my experience? Jim and John are excited for me, and I'm excited. John told me, "We're going to make sure your dream comes true."

I can say that McDonald's gave me the confidence to pursue my dream. I didn't go to school to learn English. All this, all that I have here, is because of McDonald's. It's the business that gave me the opportunity to build myself.

The story of McDonald's supervisor Jonathon is a powerful real-world example of the amazing power of accountability to transform lives.

As a sophomore in high school, I had to grow up very, very fast. I found out I was going to be a dad at sixteen years old. I knew I had to be a man. I applied to McDonald's because it was conveniently across the street from my high school. I could walk across the street from school and go to and from work. I was hired June 23, 2003. On July 1, 2003, my girlfriend gave birth six months into the pregnancy and the baby passed away. I had only worked one shift at McDonald's.

I'm a firm believer that everything happens for a reason, and I feel like that was my reason to grow up. California law states that if a fetus is thirty weeks old, you have to have a funeral for it. [Legally, a burial or cremation must happen after twenty-four weeks, but not necessarily a funeral.] My son was thirty-two weeks, so at sixteen, we had to plan a funeral for our baby. It was the hardest thing I ever did in my life.

After the baby died, I thought, I have the job. I'm going to see what happens here. The manager who hired me transferred right after I started. A new manager took over, and right away, he and I were like oil and water. I think he saw me as a young punk who thought he knew everything. Honestly, I thought I did at that point! So he only gave me one three-hour shift a week. I was the Saturday morning hashbrown person. I didn't fight the hours. I didn't need the job because I had no expenses. I was living at home.

Then, a few months later, my mom kicked me out of my house. For about three weeks, I didn't have anywhere to go. I was sleeping at different friends' houses. I slept in my car one night. It was a really tough time. I couldn't even wash my uniform. One day my manager told me my uniform was wrinkled so I should clock out and go home. "You can't work like that," he said. I tried to talk to him and tell him I didn't have a choice and to help me out. He didn't want to hear it. That was a different time.

It probably didn't help that, leading up to this, I really didn't care about the job. But I had to start caring real fast. I talked to my GM and asked, "Hey, what can I do to get more hours? What can I do to improve?" He told me I had to try harder, do this, this, and this. He coached me. He was very candid and straight up told me, "You're not a good worker. You don't follow procedures. You're late. Your uniform sucks. I'm going to fire you." I told him I would get better. I had to.

Shortly after, I had to start paying my friend's mom rent, which I couldn't afford. I begged my GM for more hours, and I guess I had started improving because he gave me the hours. And as odd as it sounds, because we didn't get along at all, I didn't want to let him down. I wanted to prove I wasn't just a dumb kid who didn't care. So I started coming in on time. I started noticing things. I started trying my best. I started doing everything I should have been doing. I ended up getting even more hours. One day my GM said, "You want to close? You could be a closer if you want more days and more hours." He put me on the schedule. Whatever we needed, I did.

I was working an eight-hour night shift five days a week and going to high school during the day. My grades slipped. I had nobody to push me. I had no drive for school because I was so focused on work. I wasn't planning on pursuing higher education anyway because I didn't like school.

In 2006, my supervisor told me he needed more managers. "And I can't believe I'm going to say this," he started, "but we're looking into you as one of those managers." I was a senior in high school. I couldn't believe it. I never once thought of myself in a leadership position. I just saw myself as doing the job to survive, to live until I found something better. I think that was the first time somebody saw potential in me. I'd never had anybody build me up that way. My mom was a single mother working two or three jobs so I never really saw her, and I had only met my dad once, a long time ago. A few weeks later, I started management training and became a manager.

When I had a daughter the next year, I tried even harder. I wanted to earn more so I could better her life. When I started working harder, doors started opening for me. After about a year, I was promoted to general manager at another store, even though I didn't have the credentials; I had only managed one department out of three. I hadn't managed people before and didn't know how to make a schedule. I had to "fake it 'til I make it."

I was off on my second day as GM. That evening I put my phone on silent, took NyQuil, and went to bed. When I woke up, I had forty-three missed calls from the store between midnight and 6:00 a.m. The restaurant had been robbed. I got dressed and drove to the store right away. The other managers were upset with me. One told me flat out, "You screwed up. Why didn't you answer?" Everything was roped off and the police were there looking at camera footage. It showed the robber, in all black and a ski mask, pointing a gun at the employees' heads while he emptied the safe. Thankfully, he did not shoot anyone before he left, but I felt horrible—so guilty. I was sure I was going to be demoted or fired. But instead, my supervisors talked to me about what happened. They told me I had to be available, even overnight. They said, "If we need to get ahold of you, it's for a reason."

I could only say, "I'm so sorry. I didn't know." I learned a valuable lesson. That's when I decided I have to be here for my team. I have to be a parental figure. I have to make them feel like they can come to me with things. Because the crew looks to the manager for support when bad stuff happens.

I wasn't fired. I wasn't demoted. Another year went by, and I won an award for Outstanding General Manager, which recognizes the top 10 percent of managers in the country. I won Outstanding General Manager for four years in a row, at two different locations.

I was officially promoted to supervisor in the summer of 2017. I'm still getting used to my role. I really have to be there for other people and uplift them, like my managers did for me.

Flexibility

To encourage your people to view their work as a vocation, you must also provide them with flexibility so they can excel both professionally and personally. Work is an essential part of our humanity, but ultimately, it is only a means to an end—and that end is family and relationships. One of the most striking benefits of working at McDonald's is its unparalleled flexibility. With the restaurant open almost 24/7, employees have the freedom to choose their working hours, which can be tailored to suit their lifestyles and personal commitments. This exceptional job flexibility creates a family-first work environment and enables employees to add value to their work while maintaining a healthy work-life balance.

This excerpt from an interview with Elton, a supervisor over several McDonald's locations, demonstrates how flexibility encourages employee retention.

I started working at McDonald's in May of '92, just before high school graduation. My plan was to work there for only a couple of years while I went to junior college. During that two years, I did a lot of everything. I was closing. I was working a lot of different shifts. I finished my two years at the JC, but I was enjoying what I was doing, so I stayed on. Before I knew it, '92 became 2024. And so here I am. I really wasn't looking to make a career with McDonald's. It was just supposed to be a job for a couple of years. But it became a lot more.

What I enjoyed most about McDonald's was the flexibility. I was able to easily change shifts to work with my school schedule. McDonald's allows tremendous flexibility because we're never closed. If you need to work on the weekends or don't want to work the weekends, if you need to work two o'clock in the afternoon to 11:00 p.m., you have the ability to do that. With such a huge range of hours, it was always very easy to switch up a shift and take care of the things I needed to take care of.

I ended up meeting my wife at McDonald's, which became another reason to stick around. When we had my first daughter, it was even more important to stay there—the flexibility was just incredible. It was easy for me to work different shifts and be home with my daughter. I worked a lot of nights, and my wife worked in the mornings, so we would trade off watching our daughter. Really, that is the staple of why I continued to stay: the flexibility it gave me to be available for my three daughters.

The Power of Reciprocity

Have you ever received a gift from someone that made you feel overwhelmed with gratitude and a desire to give something back? This is known as the law of the gift and shows the power of reciprocity. When someone gives us something or does something beneficial for us, we experience a sense of joy and happiness that compels us to either reciprocate or "pay it forward" to someone else. Whether a friend helps us move or a neighbor lends a hand, we often feel the urge to return the favor. This powerful exchange of generosity and kindness creates a positive chain reaction that brings meaning and purpose to our lives. As a leader, leveraging the power of reciprocity brings meaning and purpose to the workplace, which creates an atmosphere that encourages employees to begin seeing their jobs as vocations.

Reciprocity is a fundamental aspect of human social interaction and plays a significant role in building and maintaining relationships, fostering cooperation, and creating a sense of trust and goodwill. Reciprocity has many benefits, such as the following:

- **Generosity:** Acts of kindness and generosity can trigger a reciprocal response. Showing generosity to others can inspire them to be more generous in return, creating a cycle of giving.

- **Trust Building:** Reciprocity is a foundation for trust. Exchanging favors or demonstrating reliability builds trust in a relationship, creating a sense of security and mutual respect.

- **Cooperation:** In business and collaborative settings, reciprocity can lead to increased cooperation. When parties work together, both can benefit.

- **Social Responsibility:** Reciprocity is often ingrained in cultural norms and values. Many societies emphasize the importance of returning favors and helping others in times of need, creating a sense of social responsibility and community.

Understanding the power of reciprocity can help individuals and organizations create more positive and cooperative relationships. When we give to and help others, the same often comes back to us in various forms, enriching our lives and strengthening our connections with those around us.

Another excerpt from Elton's interview is a profile in the power of reciprocity.

My leadership value is first and foremost family and support. It is just trying to do the right thing, as hard as that might be sometimes in the situation. That carries a lot of weight in our field when we work with people who start as strangers. We spend a little bit of time with them. We try to get to know them. And we're also trying to get them to understand and trust in what we're trying to do, the systems we put in place, and the philosophies we promote. That's not always easy. You have to have some connection at a certain level in order for them to trust you and accept what you're trying to do.

When you can be honest and share a little vulnerability with people, you show them you are human and will eventually make that connection. They will start to believe in what you're trying to achieve. They'll trust you. If you don't make connections with your employees, it's like asking people you barely know to do something. They may not have a good idea of why you want them to do it. You'll often run into a lot of resistance. Communication is huge, and it starts with getting to know somebody.

There's almost no problem that can't be solved with an honest, face-to-face conversation. The other day, someone I've worked with for many years said during one of our conversations, "I appreciate these conversations. I appreciate you listening and understanding. This is why I am loyal and why I do what you ask, regardless of what it is or where it's at." That felt good to hear.

I have a fairly new GM. I'd seen her around other groups, very bubbly and happy all the time. Friendly and upbeat. We'd been working with each other for a few months when I came in one day and noticed her demeanor was very low. She just wasn't herself. I had already gotten to know her a little bit so was comfortable asking, "Is everything okay? You don't seem like yourself today."

"I'm not okay," she said. "I'm not getting a lot of support at home with housework and with all the kids."

I took that as an opportunity to talk a bit about it, about trying to balance her work life and personal life. "Why don't you and your husband and your kids go to a theme park and go out to a pizza place on the company? Turn in your receipts. Do that and let me know how it goes. Maybe you guys can find a way to connect, and your husband will see the value in what you do with your work."

She was very grateful. To this day, she jokes, "When can I have another GM outing?" She's come a long way since that down day.

Another example is a young lady I've worked with for eight or nine years. Again, we have a good enough working relationship that I can see when she isn't quite herself. She's reached out to me many times when she's stressed and contemplating whether she wants to continue this work. We have had some long conversations, and I've given her the ability to take some time off here and there to help her refresh her outlook.

So, it's a lot of things like that. One of my restaurants in a remote area is hard to staff. A manager there was going through some hard times during the winter. She didn't have the funds to pay her power bill. She had a family. "Let me see what I can do," I told her. We made a couple of calls and paid her bill that month. She was very grateful.

When you do things like that for people, it takes the working relationship to a whole other level. Those are the kinds of things where, all of a sudden, you're not just their employer; you're somebody that they know. You're not just a face; they know your name. You're much more than just their boss. Getting to know people and doing kind things for them breeds a family atmosphere. It breeds loyalty. It's much nicer to work in an environment like that. It makes it so much easier to get support from your people when they feel loyalty all the way around, and that loyalty starts at the top.

Elton purposefully gets to know his staff and helps them when they are in need; in return, they are loyal and hardworking. This reciprocity is what drives a hospitality culture rooted in truth and goodness. We have the capacity to give of ourselves, and that is when we ultimately find joy and fulfillment. It all starts with one hospitality moment at a time. How would your life and relationships be different if you chose to leverage reciprocity in your daily life?

Conclusion

I END THIS BOOK BY PARAPHRASING THE FAMOUS WORDS FROM Apple's iconic "Think Different" ad campaign.

Here's to the foolish. The nonconformists. The eccentrics. The disruptors. The ones who perceive the world differently. They defy rules and disdain conventionality. You can quote them, challenge them, celebrate them, or criticize them. The one thing you can't do is discount them. Because they drive change. They propel humanity forward. While some may label them as mad, we see brilliance. Because those audacious enough to believe they can transform the world are the ones who do.

We all have the power to change the world, thanks to the gift of the dignity of causality. This change happens one life at a time, and it often comes in unexpected ways and from unexpected people. Sometimes we see the effect of our actions; sometimes we don't know how our actions made a difference. But we must trust in the process and the reach of our lives. By rediscovering and applying the essential transcendental virtues of beauty, truth, and goodness to our lives and organizations, we produce an ancient antidote for the conundrum of modern management.

You have learned the difference between society-defined success and true excellence and that to lead yourself and your organization toward true excellence, you must first look closely at the shadows you cast. This begins by acknowledging the attitudes, behaviors, and actions you project onto those around you.

You read about the power of the law of attraction on the psyche and the significant influence of conformity and culture, and how you can deliberately use them to your advantage.

You learned about the damaging effects of excessive social media and were encouraged to build your antifragility by filtering the negativity but also adopting a neutral approach to your emotions. Find a way to slow down and process those emotions and then make a choice on how to bridge stimulus and response. Seek positivity, empathy, and compassion when possible—all the while understanding the fragility of others and respecting them accordingly.

You learned how to recognize, seek, and create true beauty; find and live your own truth; and express goodness based on that truth. By embodying these transcendental virtues, you begin to live a life of vocation with intrinsic value and deep meaning.

You saw one theme consistently emerge in interviews with thriving McDonald's leaders: the power of mentorship in their lives. While many successful people like to talk about their own grit and determination, the truth is that we all need help and support to achieve our goals. This is the power of community: working together to achieve excellence and helping each other along the way.

I hope this book inspires you to consider a reset—a reset in how you perceive beauty, truth, and goodness; a reset in how you process your thoughts; a reset in how you view your life's work in relation to your vocation; and a reset in how you consume social media.

I encourage you to strive to apply what you learned to your life, and specifically to your organization, every day, one day at a time. The power to create a countercultural revolution lies within you.

I hope you embrace your individuality and tap into your beauty, truth, and goodness to lead and inspire others. The aspirational word that comes to mind is *magnanimity*, from the Latin *magnus* and *animus*, meaning "greatness of soul and spirit." In a world where people crave leadership and conformity, you hold the power to fill the void and create a better future. You can take the reins and make a difference. As the saying goes, "If not us, then who? If not now, then when?" Now is the time to take the next step toward creating a better world—and you don't have to work for McDonald's to apply these ideas in your journey.

Your path will not be linear. As Steven Spielberg said, "Failure is inevitable. Success is elusive." Sometimes things may seem to fall apart; you will fail in leadership and relationships, and some days and months will be chaotic and dysfunctional. However, the meandering journey toward excellence need not be limited by the preconceived and vacillating definition of success—a definition that tends to rely on a prosperous outcome. The journey toward excellence is better seen as a continuous progression of facing your fears, faults, and failures, and life's new opportunities. During difficult moments, you must remember that tomorrow offers a new opportunity to be back on the path toward excellence—nothing more, nothing less.

As Nike stated in the 1970s, "There is no finish line."

I hope you enjoy the journey!

Afterword

THE RECURRING THEME IN THIS BOOK IS THE POWERFUL DISTINC-
tion between reaching some opaque notion of success and the
concept of intrinsic excellence, which can be traced directly to my
father. He had a self-possessed sense of self that allowed him to
define his own path of excellence in his personal and professional
life. He didn't let societal expectations or conventional ideas of
extrinsic "success" determine his life's plan. Instead, he unwav-
eringly committed to his own intrinsic excellence rather than
so-called success. With this mindset, he made choices that aligned
with his values as a husband, father, and entrepreneur regardless of
what others thought or how society at large was progressing. My
father's way of looking at life has stayed with me and has become
a guiding principle in my own life's meandering journey.

Therefore, I believe that his story, as told in his own words, is
a rightful wrap-up of my book. In 2016, EWTN Television, in
conjunction with the Catholic University of America, profiled
our company in its inaugural series titled *Business as a Force for
Good*. As part of the piece, they extensively interviewed my father,
the original patriarch of the company. It was his chance to tell his
story, and like all of our stories, it is a universal one. His chronicle
is really a metastory of millions of Americans over the past two

centuries and stands as a testament to how great this experiment in democracy has been for our nation.

An American Story:
Anthony M. Abbate (1935–2021)

Interviewer: Who do you consider you are, and what is your McDonald's story?

My father: I consider myself an entrepreneur and a family man. I believe that's the essence of who I am. If there's anything noteworthy about me, I would say that I'm willing to take risks for the sake of my family and God.

I come from an old Italian-Sicilian family. My dad immigrated to the US from the old country, and so did my mom's family, though she was born here. My dad used to talk about the missed opportunities he had when he was young. He always regretted not going into business and being his own boss. But the opportunities he had were not very big, like opening a fruit stand. After I graduated from college with an engineering degree, I started working as an engineer in a few different companies. I worked for General Electric in the past, specifically on a program involving spy satellites. Our team would put the satellites into orbit, and I was part of the analysis team responsible for monitoring the satellite's performance and identifying any issues. Once the satellite was in orbit, we would recover the film and conduct a final analysis to determine what went well and what needed improvement. Between missions, we often had periods of downtime that lasted for a few weeks.

During the down periods, my two close friends and I, who are engineers, used to discuss investments and potential business ventures. Due to our lack of business experience, we decided to explore franchising. To simplify the process, we categorized franchising into three main types: food franchises, automotive franchises, and miscellaneous franchises. We attended franchise shows and requested information from various franchises. After reviewing the information, we would discuss the advantages and disadvantages of each option. McDonald's was one of the franchises that caught my attention from the start. They were very honest and straightforward in their approach, but there was one issue: they required a full-time partner, who would have to leave his engineering career and work at McDonald's. This posed a challenge for us.

I didn't give it much thought initially because I wasn't sure where we would end up. We visited various franchises, but none of them caught our attention like the McDonald's franchise did. So, we decided to pursue it. I got in touch with McDonald's in early 1967, and they sent me to LA to interview with the regional manager. The interview was not about me interviewing them, but rather them interviewing me.

The regional manager believed that we could make it work, so I went back and had a conversation with my two partners, Joe and Frank. I explained the situation to them and the financial requirements. We needed to put in a security deposit of $4,000 to be included in the franchise list. I informed them that the franchise fee is non-interest bearing, and they could leave anytime they wanted, but they wouldn't earn any interest on their money. However, they would get their money back. This was a little frustrating, and the other guys didn't seem too keen on the idea. I explained to them that one of us would have to quit our engineering job if we decided to go into the restaurant business, and none of us were too enthusiastic about doing that. At that time, I had eight years of service with General Electric, and the others had twelve and fifteen years of experience.

At that time, I had three children, and so did one of my buddies. The other one had four children. All of us were working in engineering jobs and were financially stable. However, I was the only one who did all the research, and I was very excited about the opportunity. I strongly believed that it would be a huge success. What impressed me the most about McDonald's was that they provided real financial statements from their restaurants. Even though they had redacted the names of the restaurants and personnel, it was still possible to analyze the statements. It allowed us to identify areas where things were going well, and we could potentially earn a lot of money.

Joe and Frank declined the opportunity, saying they didn't want to take the chance. I was convinced that it was a great opportunity, but I didn't have the financial resources to do it alone. That's when I approached my single brother, Joe, and explained the situation to him. I told him that I wanted to go for this opportunity but didn't have the money to invest and asked him to be a partner with me. Initially, he refused, but eventually, he agreed to lend me the money. However, I persuaded him to be a full partner instead of just a lender, as I believed it was an excellent opportunity for both of us. "You know, no matter what happens, you'll get your full money back," I assured my potential business partner. He agreed and we went into business together, with him acting as a silent partner.

We received a few franchise offers and carefully considered each one. However, we decided against choosing options in Utah or other locations. Eventually, we were presented with an opportunity to own a franchise in California. When we initially signed up for the McDonald's opportunity a few years earlier, I had three children. But by 1969, my family had grown to include five children under six years old!

We began constructing the restaurant in September 1969. My role was to coordinate the project, hire a crew, and arrange for the necessary equipment while simultaneously trying to secure financing. However, obtaining funding was challenging as most banks were not interested in financing restaurants or used restaurant equipment. Since McDonald's did not offer financing, we had to find our own source of funding. Eventually, I was able to secure a loan from a bank to cover the additional costs that we couldn't afford. I stayed at the site from August until we opened the restaurant in December. I used to drive home on weekends while staying here on weekdays, leaving Jane to take care of our five kids alone. She did an outstanding job, taking care of everything from arranging the sale of our house to managing the move to our new home. In December, my wife, Jane, and our kids came to stay with me. Unfortunately, we faced difficulty finding a home to rent due to our large family size. Consequently, we decided to purchase a house instead. However, upon moving in, Jane encountered a few problems, such as the lack of heating and a house number. She improvised and used a crayon to write the house number. Nevertheless, we were able to overcome these challenges and successfully launch our business from the very first day.

The restaurant was successful right from the start, but we faced some problems that most restaurant businesses encounter due to undercapitalization. My wife, Jane, and I had decided to go at least a year without any income. Our lifestyle was simple, and being an old Italian, I was used to eating low-cost meals like pasta dishes. This is how I got into McDonald's, and I was fortunate to get in early. Our store number was 1313, while there are over thirty-five thousand stores today.

On our first day of opening, we were all filled with excitement. Jane was there with our kids, except for Bobby, our youngest one, who was absent from the family picture taken at the restaurant. Even today, he still feels upset about it. Jane was not only looking after our five children but also did the first payroll for the store, which had about forty staff members at that time. We had uniforms, and she used to wash them all for the kids. Most of our employees were kids, but we also had some airmen working with us. Though it was an exciting time, it was also challenging.

It goes back to the dream my father had of taking a chance when he was young. It could have been a fruit stand that worked out, or it could have failed. When I had my opportunity, it wasn't an easy decision because I only gave myself two years. If it didn't work out in two years, I had to switch careers because the engineering profession changes so rapidly. You can become obsolete if you're away from it for three to four years. But it was worth it. I just wanted to do it, and I couldn't have done it without the support of my wife. From the first time I mentioned it to her, she never said one negative thing. However, my two engineering buddies and their wives were just the opposite. They couldn't understand why I was even thinking about leaving engineering.

The family business was truly a family affair. Even before the children were old enough to come down to the restaurant and do menial jobs like scraping gum and picking up trash, I would have them come into my office and help distribute promotional cards. These cards were good for a hamburger or other items, and I had my young children sort through the paperwork from the restaurant, separate the cards, and put them in a pile. As they grew older, I had them do more tasks like picking up trash, cigarettes, and papers around the restaurant. When they turned fourteen, they started working at the restaurants after school and around their schedules, if they were involved in sports. They also worked during the summer. However, they also had responsibilities at home, which I felt was important to maintain.

I don't think my sons work as hard as I did, but they have a different approach. They are more into high-tech solutions. They can use computers to gather information and produce printouts. They are just as dedicated as we were, but they work in a different way.

Overall, it has been a wonderful career and I feel blessed to have done this with family and have had all the support from my wife along the way.

About the Author

Author, speaker, and McDonald's owner/operator **JOHN ABBATE** has three passions: faith, family, and business. He holds a BBA in economics from the University of San Diego, an MBA with a concentration in finance from the University of Notre Dame's Mendoza School of Business, an MA in Catholic theology from the Augustine Institute, and an MSL from Wake Forest University School of Law.

John serves and supports numerous local and regional nonprofit initiatives. As an owner of numerous McDonald's restaurants throughout the central San Joaquin Valley of California, John is a well-known public speaker on business theory, brand strategy, entrepreneurship, leadership, and business ethics. He has received numerous operations, people, and leadership awards over the years and has held several leadership positions within the greater owner/operator community, focusing on regional and national marketing, operations, and supply chain. John is co-founder of Possibility Productions, a provider of faith-based inspirational speaking and music events, and author of *Invest Yourself: Daring to Be Catholic in Today's Business World*.